Inuinnaqtun English

....

Dictionary

Edited by Gwen Angulalik

Tuglirmik Titiraqhimajuq
Second Edition

This dictionary is the result of a coordinated initiative between Nunavut Arctic College, Nunavut Bilingual Education Society, and Inhabit Media Inc.

Published by Inhabit Media Inc.
www.inhabitmedia.com

This project was made possible in part by the Government of Canada.

We acknowledge the support of the Canada Council for the Arts for our publishing program.

NBES

ᑲᑎᒪᔨᖏᑦ ᓄᓇᕗᑦ
Nunavut
Arctic College

ISBN 978-1-77227-374-8

Coordinated by	Neil Christopher
	Pelagie Owlijoot
	Fiona Buchan-Corey
Second Edition	
Edited by	Gwen Angulalik
	Julia Ogina
	Rosemarie Meyok
Designed by	Ellen Ziegler

Inuinnaqtun English

··

Dictionary

Edited by Gwen Angulalik

Tuglirmik Titiraqhimajuq
Second Edition

Note to Reader

In 1996, Gwen Angulalik, who grew up in Perry River and Kuugjuaq, Margo Kadlun-Jones, who grew up in Bay Chimo (Umingmaktok) and Arctic Sound, and linguist Betty Harnum, taught Inuinnaqtun at Nunavut Arctic College in Cambridge Bay. To teach the course, they adapted *Kangiryuarmiut Uqauhingita Numiktittitdjutingit*, a dictionary produced for a similar dialect in Holman Island, by Ronald Lowe and others on behalf of the Committee for Original Peoples' Entitlement in 1983. The need for an Inuinnaqtun dictionary that reflected the local dialect was soon realized. As a team, Gwen, Margo, and Betty revised the dictionary with elders Mabel Ekvana Angulalik, who grew up in the Chantry Inlet, Perry River, and Gjoa Haven area, and Frank Analok, who was raised in the Ikpigjuaq area near Cambridge Bay. In 2012, Nunavut Arctic College worked with Inhabit Media to update and reprint this dictionary. A working group, including Neil Christopher, Pelagie Owlijoot, Julia Ogina, and Fiona Buchan-Corey, worked with Gwen Angulalik to revise the original dictionary and make corrections.

In 2020, Inhabit Education's Inuinnaqtun working group (Gwen Angulalik, Julia Ogina, and Rosemarie Meyok) revised the dictionary so that it accurately reflected the orthographic standard for Inuinnaqtun they helped develop for the Government of Nunavut Department of Education. During this revision, several other improvements were made, such as refining definitions and adding key terms throughout.

Inuinnaqtun
to
English

A

aadjigiiktuk (*also* **aadjikkiiktuk)**	two identical or the same
aadjigijaa (*also* **aadjikkutaa)**	looks like him/her/it; resembles him/her/it
aadjikkiiktuk (*also* **aadjigiiktuk)**	two identical or the same
aadjikkutaa (*also* **aadjigijaa)**	looks like him/her/it; resembles him/her/it
aagut (*also* **aaktuut)**	skinning knife
aahanngiq	long-tailed duck
aahivak	spider
aajuraq	crack in winter ice that opens and then freezes
aaktuq	has skinned something
aaktuqtuq	skins something
aaktuut (*also* **aagut)**	skinning knife
aalla	the other one; a different one; another one
aallami	in/on/at a different one; elsewhere; somewhere else
aallangajuq	is different; has changed
aallannguqtuq	becomes different; changes
aallatqiiktuk	two different (things)
aallatuqtuq	commits adultery
aallaunahugijaa	mistakes him/her/it for someone/something else
aalliak	sled
aalliaqtuqtuq	travels by sled
aalliniq (*see* **qaaq, alvakhaq)**	caribou-skin mattress
aalliraq (*see* **tunmiraq, aluijarvik)**	mat made of skin (to sit on)

aalliraujaq	saucer
aanaakhiiq	whitefish
aanniaqtailiniq (*also*** pimattiarniq)**	health; being healthy; staying healthy; preventing illness; taking good care of oneself
aanniaqtuq	is sick; is ill
aanniarvik	hospital; health centre; nursing station
aanniqtuq	hurts himself/herself/itself
aannuraangijaqtuq (*also*** uhiqtiqtuq)**	undresses; takes off his/her (own) clothes
aannuraangiqtuq (*see*** uhiqtuq)**	is naked; has undressed; has no clothes on
aannuraaq	an article of clothing
aannuraaqarvik	clothes closet
aannuraaqtuq	puts on his/her/its own clothes; dresses himself/herself/itself
aannuraaqtuqtuq	dresses up; gets dressed
aannuraariiqtuq	is already dressed
aannuraat	clothes
aappak (*also*** paapak)**	father
aappakhaq (*also*** angutikhaq)**	stepfather
aaq	darn it!
aaquaq	old woman
aarluk	killer whale; timber wolf
aarluktuq	gets a killer whale; gets a timber wolf
aarlungajuq	keeps his/her/its head back; keeps his/her/its chin up
aarluqtuq	looks up; puts his/her/its head back; raises his/her/its chin
aatituuqtuq	shakes hands with... ; says hello
aavaqtuq	hunts around on foot; ventures inland
ablaangajuq	has his/her/its legs spread

abluqtuq	takes a step
abluriq	doorstep
adjijuq	haemorrhaging
adjiqijuq	spits blood
affaqpallaijuq	falls with a crash
agiaq	file; tool used in carving
agiaqtaa	files it
agiaqtuq	files something
agiraq (*also* uluaraut)	fiddle, violin
agiraqtuq (*also* uluaraqtuq)	plays a fiddle, violin
agjaqtaa	carries him/her/it; hauls him/her/it; brings him/her/it
agjaqtuq	brings something; carries something
agjautik	wheelbarrow
agliruq	jawbone
aglu	seal's breathing hole
aglualiuqtuq	makes a fishing hole
agluaq	fishing hole
agluliuqtuq	a seal makes a breathing hole
agluqtuq (*also* puuvjaqtuq)	it (animal) dives underwater; it (animal) plunges
agluraqtuq	dives repeatedly; plays in water (of persons)
ahiani	somewhere else; in a different place; in another place; elsewhere
ahiaq (*see* paun'ngaq)	fruit; berry
ahiaqtaqtuq (*see* paun'ngaqtaqtuq)	goes gathering fruit; goes berry picking
ahidjijuq	prepares berries; cleans berries
ahini	elsewhere
ahiqquq (*also* navvaq)	piece of a broken object
ahiruijuq	miscarriage

ahiruqtuq	is damaged; is broken
ahu (*also*** immaqaak)**	maybe; probably
ai	eh; right
aihiqtuq (*also*** angilraqhiqtuq)**	is homesick
aijaa	gets him/her/it; fetches him/her/it
aijuq	goes home
aik (*also*** ainnuaq)**	sister-in-law of a male
aikhiqtuq (*also*** -taq-, -tauti-, aijaa)**	fetches; goes to get something
aikhiutijaa	fetches something for him/her/it
ailaq	dampness
ailaqtuq	is damp
aingittuq	vest; has no sleeves
ainngittuq	hasn't gone home
ainniq	crack in ice that remains open in spring
ainnuaq (*also*** aik)**	sister-in-law of a male
aippaagu	next year
aippaagutqikpat	the year after next
aippaangani	last year
aippaq (*see*** inuuqati)**	spouse; companion
Aippiut	Tuesday
aiq (*d. attik/aik, pl. attit/ait***)**	sleeve
airutik	fur trim around cuffs
aittaqtuq	opens his/her/its mouth
aittauqtuq	yawns
aittiijuq	waits for someone to come home
aittuqtaa	gives him/her/it a gift
aittuqtuijuq	gives something to many persons; distributes something
aittuqtuq	gives a gift; gives something away
aittuuhiaq	a gift received

aittuuhiaqtuq	receives a gift
aittuun/aittuut/aittuuti	a gift given away; a present given away
aittuutigijaa	gives it as a gift
aiviq	walrus
aiviqtuq	gets a walrus
ajagutaq/ajakutaq	rainbow
ajakutaaq/ajagutaaq	removable stand
ajanikittuq	there is a narrow space in between
ajaniqtujuq	there is a wide space in between
ajapqumiarvik	a place to lean one's elbows
ajaraaq	string game
ajaraaqtuq	plays string games
ajaraun/ajaraut/ajarauti	string used for string games
ajuaq	a boil
ajuiqhajaa	trains him/her/it
ajulaqtuq (*see* **tiggak**)	a rutting male seal stinks
ajuqhittuq	cannot reach some place; is stuck
ajuqtuq	cannot; is incapable; is unable
ajurnaqtuq (*see* **nalunaqtuq**)	is difficult or hard
ajurnarman/ajurnarmat	it can't be helped; there's nothing you can do; it's impossible
akhaarniq	fall of stone; scree; landslide
akhaktuq	rolls
akhaluun/akhaluut/akhaluuti	truck; car; vehicle
akhaluutikkuuqtuq	goes by car/truck/vehicle
akhatquq	upper arm
akhun	try hard; go ahead; more effort; really...
akhunaaq	rope
akhuuqtuq	makes an effort; tries hard

aki	counterpart; one of two; price (what is exchanged for something of equal value); other side of a body of water
akiani	across; on the other side (of a body of water); on the opposite shore
akihaqtuq	challenges someone to a game
akiittuq	it is free; it doesn't cost anything
akiittuqtaqtuq	gets them for free
akikitqijaujuq	it is cheaper
akikittuq	it is cheap; it is inexpensive
akikittuqtaarijaa	gets it cheaper
akiliqtaa	pays for it
akiliuhiarijaa	receives it as a payment
akilliq	located at the opposite end
akimahuktuq	always wants to win
akimaittuq	loses a game
akimajuktuq	always wins
akimajuq	wins a game
akin/akit/akiti	pillow
akiraq	opponent
akiraqatigiiktuk	they (two) carry something together
akiraqtuqtaa	takes revenge on him/her/it; fights back at him/her/it
akiraqtuqtuq	fights; fights back; takes revenge
akirariik	two opponents; two enemies
akirarijaa	has him/her/it as an opponent
akiraun/akiraut/akirauti	yoke for carrying two water pails
akirautik	stretcher (for carrying an injured person)
akitujuq	is expensive
akituvallaaqtuq	is too expensive

akkiutaq	plate
aktikkutariik	two the same size
aktuqtaa	touches him/her/it
aku	tailpiece of clothing
akujuq	stirs; mixes
akukittuq	is short (clothing); has a short tailpiece (clothing)
akuliak/akuliaq (*also* kiinaq) (*see* qauq)	face
akuliarikhijuq	recovers from an illness
akuliariktuq	has a nice face
akulliq	the one in the middle
akulliqun/akulliqut/akulliquti	middle child; something that is in the middle
akulrutaaqtuq	goes in between
akun'nganiittuq	is located in between
akunniq	the space in between
akuqtujuq	is long (clothing)
akurun/akurut/akuruti	skirt
akuttijuq	punches dough; kneads dough; mixes something
akutaq	Inuit ice cream (a mixture of whipped fat, dried fish, and berries, especially aqpit)
alaiqtuq	wears out; bottom part is worn out (sole of shoe, etc.)
alappaa (*see* iidji)	I'm cold; it's very cold (weather)
alappaaqtuq (*see* qaajuqtuq)	feeling cold
algaak	a pair of gloves
algaaq	glove
algaijaqtuq (*also* algaiqhijuq)	has cold hands
algaiqhijuq (*also* algaijaqtuq)	has cold hands
algak (d. *algaak*)	hand
algaktuq	digs

algalaq	club in a deck of cards (literally a small hand)
algaujaq	starfish (literally resembles a hand)
algaun/algaut/algauti	wrist (human)
algiqhiijuq	roasts something
algiqtuq	is burnt
algirnilaqijuq	smells burnt
algu	headwind
alguangajuq	is bold, audacious, daring
alguilitaq	windscreen
algumuuqtuq	travels against the wind
aliahuktuq	is happy
alianaigijaa	is bored by him/her/it; makes fun of him/her/it
alianaittuq	is not funny; is not fun; is not enjoyable
alianaqtuq	is funny; is fun; is enjoyable
aliiquhiqtuq	is occupied; is busy; keeps himself/herself/itself busy
alikhaq	young bearded seal; bearded seal skin used to make rope
aliktaa	tears it; rips it
aliktuq	tears; rips
aliktuqtaa	tears it in several places; rips it in several pieces
alilaaqtuq	can tear, rip
alilajuq (*see* titiraakhaq, titiraq)	paper; cardboard
aliqak	older sister of a male
aliqakhaq	older stepsister of a male
aliqti *(d. aliqtik)*	long duffle sock; caribou-skin sock

allaijaijuq (*see* **allaijaqtaa, killaijaijuq, qaammiruhuktuijuq)**	mends something; patches a rip
allaijaqtaa	she/he is mending it; patching it
allaliqtuq	the sky is clearing up
allaqhijuq	wipes something
allaqtaa	wipes him/her/it
allarun/allarut/allaruti	towel
alluk (d. *allak*)	sole of a boot; sole of a foot
alraaq	afterbirth
alruhiqiji	electrician
aluaq	coal
alugvik	dog dish (a thing for lapping)
aluijarvik (*see* **tunmiraq, aalliraq)**	doormat
aluktaa	licks him/her/it once
aluktuq	licks once
aluktuqtaa	licks him/her/it repeatedly
aluktuqtuq	licks repeatedly
alurnaq	dog's paw
aluun/aluut/aluuti	spoon
aluutinnuaq	teaspoon
aluutirjuaq	tablespoon
alvakhaq (*see* **aalliniq, qaaq)**	caribou-skin mattress; bottom bed cover made of caribou skin
alvat (*see* **aalliniq, alvakhaq, qaaq)**	caribou-skin bedding
amaamak (*also* **maamak)**	mother
amaamakhaq (*also* **maamakhaq, arnakhaq)**	stepmother
amaamakhaliuqtuq	mixed milk for baby; drinking broth to produce milk
amaamaktuq (*also* **maamaktuq)**	a baby sucks milk; a baby nurses

amaamaun/amaamaut/ amaamauti (*also* maamaun)	baby bottle
amaaqtuq	carries a baby on his/her/its back; packs a baby on his/her/its back
amaruaq	young wolf; wolf
amaruq (pl. *amaqqut*)	wolf
amaulik	male common eider duck
amaulikkaaq	snow bunting (snowbird)
amaun/amaut/amauti	woman's parka for packing a baby on her back
amiakkut	pieces left over; remnants
amigaittut (*see* inugiaktut, amihut)	are many; are numerous
amihut (*see* amigaittut, inugiaktut)	many
amiijaijuq	skins something
amiiqtaa	skins it
amiiqtuq	wears out; is worn out (of clothes); is skinned
amikuq (*also* ilakuq)	leftover
amiq (d. *ammak*, pl. *amngit*)	sealskin; animal hide
amiraijaijuq	peels a fruit, vegetable
amiraijaqtaa	peels it; skins it
amiraq	peel of fruit, vegetable; skin of a fish; bark of a tree
anaanattiaq	grandmother
anaq	excrement
anaqtaun/anaqtaut/anaqtauti	sewage truck
anaqtautiliqiji	sewage truck driver
anaqtuq	defecates
anarnaut	laxative
anarvik	toilet; bathroom; washroom
anautaa	his/her club

anautaq	a club
angaadjuvik (*see* aturvik)	church
angajuaktaq	married to older spouse
angajugiik/-t	siblings of the same sex
angajuk	older sibling of the same sex; (older brother of a male; older sister of a female)
angajukhaq	older stepsibling of the same sex; (older stepsister of a female; older stepbrother of a male)
angajukhiqun	eldest sibling
angajun'nguq (*see* nukaun'nguq, ukuaq)	brother-in-law of male (husband of wife's older sister); sister-in-law of female (wife of husband's older brother)
angajuqqaaq	parent
angak	uncle on mother's side; mother's brother
angatkuq	shaman
angiglijuq	grows; gets bigger
angijuq (*also* -qpak, -rjuaq)	tall; big; superior (in size, importance, strength, etc.)
angilraqhiqtuq (*also* aihiqtuq)	is homesick
angilraqtuq	is back home
angilrarvik	home
angilraujuq	goes home
angilrauliqtuq	is on the way home
angiptak	hummock
angiqtuq	says yes (verbally or by raising eyebrows); agrees
angitigijuq	is as tall as...; is as big as...
angitqijaq	the biggest one
angivittuq/itumittuq	is taken apart
angmagiaq	capelin
angmajuq	is open

angmaniq	opening
angmaqtaa	opens it
angmaqtirun	can opener; bottle opener
anguaqtuq/anguuqtuq	propels
anguhalluq	male animal
anguhuqtuq	is a skilled hunter
angujaa	catches it (a game animal)
angujakti	warrior; soldier
angujaktut	are fighting a war
angujuq	gets a game animal; catches a game animal
angulajuq	chews a skin to soften it
angun/angut/anguti	boy; man; human male
angunahuaqti (*also anguniaqti*)	hunter
angunahuaqtuq (*also anguniaqtuq*)	hunts
anguniaqti (*also angunahuaqti*)	hunter
anguniaqtuq (*also angunahuaqtuq*)	hunts
angunnait	men's clothing
angut/angun/anguti	boy; man; human male
angutikhaq (*also aappakhaq*)	stepfather
angutituqtuq	has sex with a man
anguun/anguut/anguuti	propeller
anguuqtuq	wet oneself
ani/anik (*compare aqqaluaq*)	brother of a female
anijuq	goes out; is born
anikhaq	stepbrother of a female
anikkurijuq	(arrow, bullet, etc.) goes right through
aniqhaaktuq	breathes
aniqhaumijaaqtuq	sighing
aniqhaummiktuq	sighs

aniqtak	surely
anirniq	breath; soul
anitaa	puts him/her/it outside
aniu	snow used for making water
aniutaqtuq	fetches snow to make water
anmuktaa	lowers him/her/it
anmun/anmut	downward; to a lower area; downstream or downriver
anmuujuq (*also hituaqtuq*)	slides once; goes down; descends; goes downriver or downstream
annaktuq	escapes; is safe
an'ngajuktuqtuq (*also an'ngajuktuq*)	is out of breath
anngun/anngut/annguti (*also nirjun*)	game animal
anniruhuktuq	is stingy; won't share
annirutijaa	refuses him/her/it
annirutijaujuq	is refused something
annivik	birthday
annivilittuq	is his/her/its birthday
annudjutijut	try to make each other laugh
annuktuq	frowns; is sad
anu (*d. annuk, pl. annut*)	harness
anuhijuq	harnessed a dog
anujaa	harnesses it
anujijuq	making harnesses for dogs
anuqhaaqtuq	there is a light wind; it is breezy; it is drafty
anuqhilaqiliqtuq	is getting windy
anuqhiqtuq	is windy
anuraiqtuq	it is no longer windy; the wind has died down
anuri	wind

anurikittuq	is a little windy
anuurijuq	harnesses something (an animal)
apihimajuq (*see* **apijuq, apittuq**)	covered with snow
apijuq (*see* **apihimajuq, apittuq**)	it snowed
apiqhijuq	asks a question
apiqhuiji	judge of a court
apiqhuijuq	asks for information
apiqhuivik	court; courtroom
apiqhuqtuq	asks; questions; interrogates
apiqhuun/apiqhuut/apiqhuuti	a question
apiqun/apiqut/apiquti	the first snow in fall
apirijaa	asks him/her/it
Apitilirvia	September
apittaaq (*see* **apittiuvik**)	polar bear den
apittiujuq	hibernates
apittiuvik (*see* **apittaaq**)	hibernation place; polar bear den
apittuq (*see* **apijuq, apihimajuq**)	is covered in snow
apkaluktaqtuq	taps (makes a noise)
apquhaaqtaa	drops by on his/her/its way
apquhiniq	trail; path
apquhiuqtuq	makes a road
apqun/apqut/apquti	road
apqutailliutaujuq	is in the way
apqutaiqtuq	there is no more roadway; there is no longer a road
apqutaittuq	there is no road
apqutiniktaa	makes room for him/her/it to pass
aptunikittuq	takes small steps
aptuniqtujuq	takes large steps

apun/aput/aputi	fallen snow
apuqtuq (*see* tulaktuq)	docking; a boat lands
apurvik (*see* niudjivik, tulagvik)	dock; landing place for boat; a place to disembark
apurvikhaqhiuqtuq	looks for a place to land a boat
aputaijaijuq	takes the snow off someone or something
aputaijaqtaa	takes the snow off him/her/it
aputtaaq/ukharjuk	snowbank
aqagu	tomorrow
aqagu X-munngaqpan/-qpat/ -qqan/-qqat	tomorrow at ___ o'clock
aqaguani	day after tomorrow
aqajat	seaweed
aqamaktuk	plays the arm pulling game
aqhaaqtaa	takes it away from him/her/it; seizes him/her/it; grabs him/her/it; snatches him/her/it
aqhaaqtaujuq	is snatched; is seized; is grabbed; is taken away from him/her/it
aqhaktuq	plays football
aqhalialaqijuq (*also* aqhalingialaqijuq)	the northern lights are out; the aurora borealis is visible
aqhaliaq/-t (*also* aqhalingiaq)	northern lights; aurora borealis
aqhalingialaqijuq (*also* aqhalialaqijuq)	the northern lights are out; the aurora borealis is visible
aqhalingiaq (*also* aqhaliaq)	northern lights; aurora borealis
aqhaluktuq	it is drafty indoors
aqiamuk	lower part of belly or abdomen
aqiaruaqtuq	starves to death
aqiaruijaijuq (*see* hunagaijaijuq)	guts a fish/game animal
aqiaruijaqtaa	guts it
aqiaruq (*see* nadjak)	stomach

aqiarurliqtuq (*also* **aqiarurliuqtuq, naarliuqtuq, nadjagliqtuq**)	has a stomach ache
aqiarurliuqtuq (*also* **aqiarurliqtuq, naarliuqtuq, nadjagliqtuq**)	has a stomach ache
aqiattuqtuq	is satiated; is full after eating
aqiatuhuktuq	still feels full
aqiaviniq	skin and flesh of the belly
aqilgiq	rock ptarmigan
aqilgivik	willow ptarmigan
aqilluqqaq	fresh soft snow
aqilummaaq	tender meat
aqittuq	is tender or soft
aqpahijuq	starts running
aqpajuaqtuq	runs away
aqpaluarutijuk	races
aqpattuq	runs
aqpik	cloudberry; salmonberry (named for its colour)
aqqaluakhaq (*compare* **anikhaq**)	younger stepbrother of a female
aqqaluaq (*compare* **ani**)	younger brother of a female
aqtuliqtuq	is an invalid; is unable to manage alone; is too weak to manage alone
aqu	stern of a boat; rear part of a boat
aquani	in the stern; in the rear part of a boat
aqublingajuq/aqubliqtuq	is crouched down
aquihimajuq	visitor from out of town
aquijuq	visits from out of town
aqumuktuq	goes to the stern of a boat
aquti	driver; pilot; captain of a boat

aquttuq

aquttuq	drives a vehicle; pilots a plane; steers a boat
aquun/aquut/aquuti	rudder
ariujaa	is fed up with him/her/it; has had enough of him/her/it
arja	ash
arjaijarvik (*see* arjakuurvik)	ashbin
arjakhaq	gunpowder
arjakuurvik (*also* higaakuvik) (*see* arjaijarvik)	ashtray
arjiqtaq	blue
arlingnaqtuq	is amazing; is unexpected
arnaaqutaq/arnalluq	female dog; bitch
arnakhaq (*also* amaamakhaq, maamakhaq)	stepmother
arnalluq	female animal
arnannait	women's clothing
arnaq	woman
arnaqati	male or female cousin on mother's side
arnaqhiun/arnaqhiut/ arnaqhiuti	woman's belonging; thing for women
arnaqtuqtuq	has sex with a woman
arnaruhiq	teenage girl
arnarvik (*compare* attak)	aunt; mother's sister (not father's sister)
arnauniriik	married couple
arnautqiik	mating pair of animals; mates
arniqijuq	goes after a woman
arvaaq (*see* arviq)	young bowhead whale
arvak	side of the hand
arvinilik	six
arvinilik atauhiq	seven
arvinilik malruk	eight

arvinilik pingahut	nine
arviq (*see* arvaaq)	bowhead whale
arviqtuq	gets a bowhead whale
ata	listen; hush
ataaguuqtaa	passes under him/her/it
ataani	under; underneath; beneath
ataatattiaq	great-grandfather
ataattiaq	grandfather
ataiqtuq	comes apart; comes loose
atajuq	added on; jumpsuit
atanikittuq	short portage
ataniq	manager; boss; God
atan'ngujaq	is demanding
atataq	amulet
atauhiinnaq	only one; the only one
atauhiq	one
atauttikkun	in unison; all together
atauttikkuuqtut	are doing something together; are doing something at the same time
atauttimuktait	puts them together
atigi	parka
atiq (pl. *atqit*)	name
atiqat (*also* atiqat/atiqatigiik)	two people named after the same person
atiqtujuq	person whose actions or words are the same as his/her namesake
atiqtuq (*see* mauliqtuq, nikpaqtuq)	goes walking on the ice to hunt seals (with guide dogs)
atiqujaanga (*see* maulgaqujaanga, nikpaqujaanga)	he/she tells me to go walking on the sea ice to hunt seals
atirluaqtuq (*also* atiruaqtuq)	a name that is given that is mocking him/her

atirluktuq

atirluktuq	a name that must be changed because a child's spirit will not accept it
atiruaqtuq (*also* **atirluaqtuq**)	a name that is given that is mocking him/her
atkaqtuq	is allowed to disembark; is let off a vehicle or boat; is dropped off
atpa	murre
atqaqtuq (*also* **atqaujuq**)	goes down; comes down; steps down from...
atqaujuq (*also* **atqaqtuq**)	goes down; comes down; steps down from...
atqin/atqit	your name; names (plural)
atqun/atqut/atquti	little stick used to trim the wick of a traditional lamp (qulliq)
atqunaqtuq	gets lots (of game)
atqunarnirujuq	the one who gets the most
attak (*compare* **arnarvik**)	aunt (father's sister, not mother's sister)
attariktuq	is flat
attiaq (*see* **atiq, haunittiaq**)	a person named after a close relative
attiqtaa	gives him/her/it a name
attiqtuijuq	says the names of things; recites the names of things
atuaqtaun/atuaqtaut/ atuaqtauti	axe
atugaq (pl. *atukkat*)	debt
atukkiqtuq	has debts
atungaq (d. *atungak*)	boot sole made from sealskin
atungaujaq (*see* **uqaujaq**)	willow leaf (looks like a boot sole)
atuqtaa	uses it; sings it
atuqtitaa	lends something to him/her/it
atuqtuq (*also* **-tuq-**)	uses

atuqtuq (*see*** ingiuqtuq, huqullaaqtuq)**	sings
atuqtuujaq	record album; CD; cassette tape; musical instrument
atuqtuujaqtuq	music is playing
aturvik (*see*** angaadjuvik)**	church (singing place)
atuun/atuut/atuuti	music; record; song; hymn
augiaq	blood clot
auglaqijuq	nose started bleeding
auguiqtuq (*see*** aunaaruiqtuq)**	stops bleeding
aujaq	summer
aujijaqtuqtuq	goes to spend the summer
aujijuq	spends the summer
aujuq	is rotten; is ripe
auk	blood
aukhiqtuq	is warming up from being cold
aukhiqtuqtuq	warms himself/herself/itself
aukhiriaq	sugar (that which melts)
aukhittiaqhimaittuq	is not quite thawed
aukhittiaqhimajuq	is properly thawed
auktirun/auktirut/auktiruti	soldering iron
auktuqtaaqtuq	is already thawed out
auktuqtaqtuq	warms up; thaws easily
auktuqtuq	melts; thaws
auktuttiaqhimaittuq	is not completely thawed
auladjun/auladjut/aulattidjut	jiggling rod; jigging rod (for jigging fish)
aulajuq	moves in one spot
aulattiji	manager; supervisor
aulattijuq	jigs for fish; is fishing at a fishing hole; is jigging for fish
aullaqhimajuq	stays out in camp; is away (out of town)

aullaaqtuq	travels
aullaqhimakhaaqtuq	has been gone for a long time
aullaqtuq	departs; leaves
aullautijaa	takes him/her/it along on a trip
aulvik (*see quglugiaq*)	hairy caterpillar
auma *(pl. aumait)*	live coal; ember
aumaallaktuq (*see uunaqtuq*)	is hot (sweating)
aumajuq	is thawed out
aumaliuqtuq	is turning to embers/coals; is red hot; burning wood
aunaaqtuq	bleeds; menstruates
aunaaruiqtuq (*see auguiqtuq*)	stops bleeding (menstruating)
aunginnannguqtuq	is covered with blood
aupadjaktuq	blushed/turned red
aupajaaqtuq	red
aupajaavjaktuq	pink
aupajangajuq/aupajangattuq	orange (the colour)
auttuq	he/she is dealing a deck of cards
auviq (*also qarmakhaq*)	snowblock
auviuqtuq (*also qarmakhaliuqtuq*)	cuts snowblocks
auvvivik (*also qarmakhaqtarvik*)	place to cut snowblocks (from the right kind of snow)
avaalaqiaq (*see uqpik*)	willows tied together to make a bedding mattress or drying rack over the qulliq
avaliittuq	is alone
avalliq (*also ungahitqijaq*)	the one that is farthest away
avataani	around; beyond
avataaqtaqtut	skipping
avatait	limbs of the body; extremities
avguaqhijuq (*also avguqhijuq*)	is cutting meat

avguijuq	cuts something up; slices something; divides it up
avgun/avgut	instrument to cut something
avguqhijuq (*also* avguaqhijuq)	is cutting meat
avguqtaa	slices it; cuts it up
avguumattiarniq	share equally; be fair
avguutijaa	to cut it up for him/her
avikhijuq	to cut off a piece
aviktaa	cuts it in half; divides it in two
aviktuijuq	is cutting into many pieces
avin'ngaaq	baby lemming
avin'ngaq	lemming
avitaa	divorces him/her; separates from him/her
avittuk	two are separated; two are divorced
avittuq	is divorced; is separated; leaves a group; leaves his/her/its relatives

haamirun/haamirut/haamiruti	apron
haattuq	is face to face with...; faces something; is flat
haavitaa	launches it (a boat)
haavittuq	drifts away; is launched
haavraq	red phalarope (drifter)
hadja (*also* tadja)	now
hadjagu (*also* tadjagu) (*see* uvattiagu)	in a few minutes; soon; shortly

hadjaguttauq (*also* **tadjaguttauq)**	be right back
haimmiqiji	foster parent
haimmiqijuq	foster parenting
haimmiqut	foster child
hain'ngihuktuq (*also* **hain'ngiguhuktuq/hain'ngijuq/ hain'riguhuktuq) (***see* **hangiaktuq)**	is regretful; jealous
haitai (*also taitai***)**	more; some more; again (childish language)
haitaiffaaqtuq (*also* **pijumaffaaqtuq, taitaiffaaqtuq)**	wants more (childish language)
hakhagiaq	redpoll (small bird)
haki	father-in-law; mother-in-law
hakiak	father-in-law and mother-in-law
hakiaq	breastbone
hakugiittuq	is weak; is not strong
hakugiktuq	is strong
hallaaqtuq	is just lying around
halraqtuk	they (two) bark at each other aggressively
halraqtuq	barks (agressively)
halumailruq	a dirty spot; a stain
halumaittuq	is dirty
halumajuq	is clean
haluuqtuq	says hello
hamani	here
hamanirmiut	people from here
hamma	these right here
hamna	this place; here
hamunga	(place it) over here
hamunngauliqtuq	is coming here
Hanahuilrun/Hanahuilrut	Sunday

hanajaa	fixes it; works on it; makes it; repairs it
hanaji	traditional term for midwife; the one that washes/cleans mother and baby when baby is born; carpenter, construction worker
hanajuq (*see*** havaktuq)**	fixes something; works on something; makes something
hanalrutit	tools
Hananngaut (*also*** Hivulliq)**	Monday
hanaqijuq	is busy
hangiaktuq (*also*** hain'ngihuktuq/ hain'riguhuktuq; hain'ngiguhuktuq; hain'ngijuq)**	is jealous
hangujuq	wanders; changes direction
hangutitaqtuq	zigzags
hani (*see*** haniraq)**	side
haniani	beside him/her/it
haniqpaijuq	brings it somewhere else
haniraq (*see*** hani)**	side
hanirarmik	wood plane (a tool for shaving wood)
hanirarmiktuq	uses a wood plane (a tool for shaving wood)
hanmijuq	faces something/someone; is against something/someone
hanmitijuk	(two) are against each other; are opposed to each other; are facing each other; are interested in each other
hannaijaqtuq (*also*** itqanaijaqtuq; parnaijaqtuq; upalungaijaqtuq)**	gets ready
hannaiqtuq	is ready; has finished working
hanngiutit	your boy/girlfriend

hanningajulik	a cross
hanningajuq	sideways
hapun/haput/haputi	fish weir
haputaq avataagut	fence that surrounds an area
haqalikitaaq	butterfly
haqanakhiut (*also* hiratittit; hiqanakhiut/hiqanakhiun/ hiqanakhiuti) (*see* ipualik)	frying pan
haqiktaqtuq	he or she sweeps; he or she rakes
haqiktaun/haqiktaut/ haqiktauti	rake; broom
haqpik	tail of a whale
haqpingajuq	when someone puts boots or shoes on the wrong feet
hatku	sharp tool
hatqiqtuq	shows up; comes into sight; appears
hatqummiqhijuq	brings something/someone into view
hatqummiqtaa	shows it; puts it in view; displays it; brings it into sight
hatqummiqtuq	shows up; comes into sight; appears
haujaa	buries it
haulluqtuq	takes the marrow out of a bone
haulluun/haulluut/haulluti	tool to take the marrow out of a bone
haumiani	on his/her/its left
haumik	left side
haumimni	on my left side
haumingmuuqtuq	is left-handed; goes to the left
haumingni	on your left side
hauniq	eggshell; pit or stone of a fruit; bone

haunittiaq (*see* atiq, attiaq, atiqat, atiqatigiik)	same name but named after different people
haunittiariik	two persons having the same name
havagluqutainnannguqtuq	needs frequent repairs
havakti	worker; employee
havaktuq	works
Havangnairvik (*also* Saaluti)	Saturday
havaqati	co-worker
havgun/havgut/havguti	stick to measure the depth of snow
havihuk	iron; metal
havik	knife (general term)
havikhaq (*also* havilhaq)	brass
havilhaq (*also* havikhaq)	brass
haviqquujaq	rice
havraq	current (ocean)
havruut	traditional tool for planing
havvariktuq	works well
havvarluktuq	works poorly or badly
havviqun	hacksaw
higaakhaq	cigarette paper
higaakuvik (*also* arjakuurvik)	ashtray
higaaq	cigarette
higaaqtuq	smokes a cigarette
higaarjuaq	cigar
higaarluk	marijuana
higaarluktuq	smokes marijuana
higguk (*see* qingaq)	beak; snout
higguqquqtujuq	long-beaked; long-nosed; long-snouted
higjaaq	tarpaulin; skin used to cover a sled

higjaq	ocean shore
higjariaq	white-rumped sandpiper (a shorebird)
hii/iihi'	yes
hiipangnittuq (*also* tariurnittuq)	salty
hiirnaqtuq	is sweet; sweet food
hiitquaq	kneecap
hiitquaqtuq	hurts his/her/its knee
hiitqumingajuq	is kneeling
hiitquq	knee; seal's rear flipper
hiitquqtuq	gets down on his/her knees
hiku	ice (on a pond, lake, ocean)
hikuaqtuq	ice is forming; there is thin ice; young ice
hikuarniq (*also* qurlurniq, kuhirniq)	icicle
hikuliaq	bottle; glass
hikulihaaq	recently formed ice
hikunngiqtuq (*also* hikun'ngiqtuq/hikun'riqtuq)	closes his/her/its eyes
hikun'ngiqtuq (*also* hikunngiqtuq/hikun'riqtuq)	closes his/her/its eyes
hikun'riqtuq (*also* hikun'ngiqtuq/hikunngiqtuq)	closes his/her/its eyes
Hikutirvia	November
hikuun/hikuut/hikuuti	container for ice
hila	outside; the outdoors; weather; mythical character Hila; knowledge
hilahiun/hilahiut/hilahiuti	barometer
hilalliq	the outermost layer
hilami	outside; in the outdoors
hilamiittuq	is outside; is outdoors

hilaqqiqtuq	the weather is really nice
hilarjuaq	skies; world
hilarluk (*also* hilaluk)	bad weather; storm
hilarluktuq (*also* hilaluktuq)	is bad weather; is stormy
hilataagut	by the outside
hilataani	on the outside of him/her/it
hiluqhijuq	inhaled
hiluraqtuq	takes a sip
hilviaq	hipbone
himmauhiqtaa	replaces him/her/it; takes his/her/its place; trades it; exchanges it
hinaa	edge of lake, sea, river; shore; edge
hinaaguuqtuq	goes along the shore of a lake, sea, river
hinaani	at the edge of a lake, sea, river; on the shore of a lake, sea, river
hinaaqhijuq	falls asleep
hingaijuq	is pregnant
hingik	point of land jutting out into a body of water; peninsula
hingiq	shoelace
hingirniq	ankle
hinigvik	bedroom; place to sleep
hinikhaaqtuq	sleeps for a long time
hinikhaq	fur trim on a parka
hiniktuq	sleeps
hinmiutaq	big char
hinnakhaqtuq	trying to go to sleep
hinnaktuqtuq	dreams
hinnakturni	in your dreams
hinnariktuq	sleeps well; sleeps soundly

hinnarluktuq	didn't sleep well/bad dream
hiqanakhiut/hiqanakhiun/ hiqanakhiuti (*also* **hiratittit**; **haqanakhiut**) (*see* **ipualik**)	frying pan
hiqiniq	sun
hiqiniq pulaliqtuq	sun sets
hiqinnaaqtuq	the sun is shining brightly
hiqiqtuq	makes a splash
hiqiraqtuq	splashes repeatedly
hiqqaqtuq	a wave crashes
hiqquut/hiqquun/ hiqquqtidjun/hiqquqtidjut (*also* **hiqquqtiun/hiqquqtidjuti**)	gun; rifle
hiqulaaq	biscuit
hiqummiktuq	shattered
hiquqtaa	shoots him/her/it with a gun
hiquqtuq	shoots with a gun
hiquriaqtaa	shoots at him/her/it; fires at him/ her/it
hiquriaqtuq	shoots at...; fires a gun
hiratittit (*also* **hiqanakhiut/ hiqanakhiun/hiqanakhiuti**; **haqanakhiut**) (*also* **ipualik**)	frying pan
hitaakiq *(d. hitaakik)*	stocking (borrowed from English)
hitamat	four
Hitammiut	Thursday
hiti	burrow
hitiliuqtuq	digs a burrow
hitkik	diamond in a deck of cards
hittuqittuq	swallows the wrong way; chokes while drinking; spits up
hituaqattaqtuq	sliding (playing)
hituaqtuq (*also* **anmuujuq**)	slides down
hituaqtuutit	sled; toboggan

hitujuq	pants have fallen down
hituliqtuq	pants are falling down
hiudjariktuq	has good hearing
hiudjarluktuq	is hard of hearing
hiulliuqtuq (*also* **hiulluktuq**)	has an earache
hiulluktuq (*also* **hiulliuqtuq**)	has an earache
hiun/hiut/hiuti (d. *hiutik*)	ear
hiuraq	sand
hiurjuk	Primus stove
hiurjuktuuq	small fish
hiurjuun/hiurjuut/hiurjuuti	grub box
hivajaaqtuq	keeps on ringing (one long ring)
hivajaqtaaqtuq	rings
hivajaqtuq	rings once
hivajaun/hivajaut/hivajauti	bell; alarm; buzzer (phone)
hivu	front part of something; the future; what lies ahead
hivuani	before him/her/it; in front of him/her/it
hivuaq	tooth; front incisor
hivuliqti	lead dog; leader
hivuliqtiliuqtuq	trains someone/something to be a leader
hivulirijaa	it; is ahead of him/her/it
hivulliq	the first one
Hivulliq (*also* **Hananngaut**)	Monday
hivullirmik	first of all
hivulliujuq	is the first; is ahead of others
hivumun/hivumut	ahead; to the future
hivunikhaqhiuqtuq	decides; makes plans; leads the way

hivuniq	front; before; that which has gone before (past); that which lies before (future); destination
hivuniqhipkaqtaa	explains to him/her/it; makes him/her/it understand
hivunniriiqtuq	has already made up his/her/its mind
hivuralik (d. hivurallak)	fancy boot; mukluk with fancy shin piece
hivvuqtaa	wrings it out
hivvuqtuijuq	wrings something out
huiqtuq	dies; passes away
huittuq	not here
hukangajuq (also kapittuq)	is tight; tight clothing
hukatirun/hukatirut/hukatiruti	wrench
hukattuq	is tight
hukhamun/hukhamut	what for; why
hukkijaaqtuq	European-style dance
hukkinaaq (also hukkinnaaq)	stroud (a woolen material)
huli	still (duration); more of...
hulijakhaq	what to do with it?
hulijakhaqhiuqtuq	is looking for something to do
huliva	what is he/she/it doing
hulivin/hulivit	what are you doing
huluk (see mitquq)	long feather of tail or wing
humi	where; in what place
humiitpa	where is he/she/it
humik/humin	what (used as the direct object of a sentence)
humiliqaak	somewhere
humin/humik	what (used as the direct object of a sentence)
humin/humit	from where

humiutauvin/humiutauvit	where are you from
humun/humut	to where
humunngaqqa	what time is it; where did he/she/it go
humunngauliqqin/-qit (*also* **humunngauvin/-vit**)	where are you going
huna (d. *hunak,* pl. *hunat*)	what
hunagaijaijuq (*see* **aqiaruijaijuq**)	guts a fish
hunagait	fish guts
hunagaq	bile
hunamiaqtuq (*see* **qutaktuq**)	comes back empty-handed (from hunting, fishing)
hunamun/hunamut	where to; in which direction
hunauva	what is it
hunauvva	alas; so; what a surprise
hungajaaqtuq	green (resembles bile)
hungajangajuq	greenish-yellow (somewhat resembles bile)
hungaq	gall bladder; bile
hunngittuq	it's nothing/unseen; a spirit
huqqaq	baleen
huqullaaqtuq (*see* **atuqtuq, ingiuqtuq**)	sings
huraaqhiuqtuq	hunts small game
hurjuktuq	confronts; attacks
hurluk	nose; nasal cavity
hurluqtuuq (*see* **mitiq**)	common eider duck (female)
huukiaq (*see* **naunaqquq**)	I wonder why; I don't know why; for whatever reason
huunngittuq	it's nothing; there's nothing there
huuq	why; what's the matter
huvaiqtuq	takes the eggs out of a fish
huvak	fish eggs; roe

i'; ih (*see* imannaq)	no (slang)
iblungajuq/iplungajuq	bowlegged
idjuaqhijuq/igjuaqhijuq	mocks someone or something by doing imitations
idjuaqtaa/igjuaqtaa	imitates him/her/it; copies him/her/it
igalaaq	window
iggiaq	throat
iggiarliqtuq/iggiarliuqtuq	has a sore/infected throat
igitaa	throws it away
igjuk *(d. igjuuk)*	testicle
iglahiktuq	burst out laughing
iglaqtittijuq	makes people laugh; is comical
iglaqtuq	laughs
iglautigijaa	laughs at him/her/it
igliaq	uterus; womb
igliq	bed
iglu	snowhouse; house
iglua	one of a pair; his/her house
igluaq	room
igluaqtaa	shot it on the side
igluaqtuq	shoots to the side
iglugiik	a pair
igluittuq	one of a pair is missing; has no house
igluktuqtuq	uses both of a pair/both hands
igluliqiji	house maintenance person
igluliuqti	house builder

iglupiaqtuqtuq	uses only one of a pair/one hand
igunaq	aged seal/walrus fat; aged seal/walrus meat in fat
iguttaq	bee
ihajuq	moulting bird; bird losing its feathers (can't fly)
ihaqutaq (pl. *ihaqutait*)	branch of a tree
iharuq (d. *ihaqquk*, pl. *ihaqqut*)	wing (of bird, plane, fly, mosquito)
ihiq	smoke; dust; steam
ihiriaq	smoke from a forest fire
ihivjuktuq	speaks with a low voice; whispers
ihivjuraq	coiled spring
ihivriuqhiji	researcher; examiner; judge of quality
ihivriuqhijuq	judges something for quality; examines something; researches something; studies something
ihivriuqtaa	judges him/her/it for quality; examines him/her/it; researches him/her/it; studies him/her/it
ihuani	at the end of it; at its extremity
ihuaqhijaa	corrects it; fixes it
ihuaqtuq	is correct; is right
ihuinaaqtuq	did wrong; crime
ihuittuq	is wrong; is incorrect
ihuma	mind; thought; idea
ihumaalugijaa	is concerned about him/her/it; worries about him/her/it
ihumaaluktuq	worries; is concerned
ihumagijaa	thinks about him/her/it
ihumagijauttiarniq	respect; be respected; be well thought of
ihumaittuq	is absent-minded
ihumajuq	thinks

ihumakittuq/ihumarluktuq	is mentally disabled; is thoughtless
ihumaliuqtuq	thinks about something; considers; makes a decision; comes up with an idea
ihumangnik	it's up to you (singular); you decide; it's your decision; it's your choice; your thought
ihumatujuq	very smart; intelligent
ihummarluktuq	has bad thoughts; mentally disabled
ihunngaq	Arctic skua (also called an Arctic jaeger)
ihuuq	trout
ihuuqiq	big lake trout
ihuuriktuq	medium-sized lake trout
iidji (see alappaa)	extreme cold (outside)
iidjilaqijuq (see alappaa)	the weather is very cold
iidjiraaluk	the weather is extremely dry and cold
Iidjirurvia	February (it gets really cold)
iigijaa	stares at him/her/it; looks attentively at him/her/it
iigijuq	looks attentively; stares
iigluktuq	has poor eyesight
iihijuq	swallows something
iijaa	swallows it
iiluktuq	has a sore eye
iiqhijuq	hid something
iiqtaa	hides him/her/it; puts it out of view
iiqtuq	hides
iiqtuqtuq	conceals himself/herself/itself; hides himself/herself/itself
ijarluktuq	has sore eye(s)

ijaruqtuq	hurts his/her/its eye; pokes his/her/its eye
ijaruvak	pupil of the eye
iji	eye
ijik	pair of eyes
ijukkaqtuq (*also* iukkaqtuq)	falls
ikaaqtaa	goes across it; crosses over it
ikaaqtuq (*see* itivjaaqtuq)	goes across; crosses over
ikaaraq (*see* pilagiaq)	crossing (a place to cross); isthmus
ikajuqtaa	helps him/her/it
ikajuqti	helper
ikajuqtuq	helps
ikhikhaq	solid colour bias tape
ikhiq (*see* qupak)	trim on a cloth parka cover
ikhivajuq	is sitting; is seated
ikhivautaq	chair
ikhivavik	living room
ikhun (*also* kikhuutit)	Arctic heather (fire starter)
iki	open wound
ikidjuk	turn it on; light it
ikijaa	puts him/her/it on board
ikijuq	gets on board; embarks
ikilik	is wounded; has a wound
ikimajuq	is on board
ikipkaqtaa	sets fire to him/her/it; helps him/her/it on board
ikitaa	lights it
ikitaqtuq	starts a skidoo, truck, etc.; fires up an engine
ikittaaqtuq	is flammable
ikittaun	electrical switch
ikittijuq	lights a fire

ikittuq	is on fire; is burning
ikittut	a few; they are on fire; they are burning
ikkalruq/itkalruq	shallow water; reef; sandbar
ikkattuq/itkattuq	the water is shallow
ikkikhan/ikkikhat/ikkikhati/ ikkikhaun(t)	wood alcohol; medicinal alcohol (not for drinking)
ikkin/ikkit/ikkiti (pl. *ikkitit*)	match; lighter
ikkitautikhaq (*see ikuallautikhaq*)	fire starter
ikpan/ikpat/ikpati	table
ikpataujaq	small table; coffee table
ikpiguhuktuq	senses something; feels something; is affected; is impacted
ikpiguhungniq (*see ikpingnarniq*)	feeling; emotion; sensation
ikpingnaqtuq	important
ikpingnarniq (*see ikpiguhungniq*)	impact; effect; result; consequence; impression
ikualaaqtuq (*see ikumajuq*)	is burning
ikualajuq	burns up; burns down
ikuallaktuq	starts burning
ikuallautikhaq (*see ikkitautikhaq*)	something to start a fire with
ikuhik	elbows
ikuhingmiktaa	pokes him/her/it with his/her/ its elbow
ikuhingmingaaqtuq	leans on his/her/its elbows
ikuhiq	elbow
ikuhiun/ikuhiut/ikuhiuti	sling for the arm
ikumajaaq (*also qilluqiqtuq*)	lightning
ikumajuq (*see ikualaaqtuq*)	is turned on; is burning; is lit
ikumaniq	flame
ikummat	candle

ikuttiaqtuq	hurts his/her/its elbow
ikuutaq	drill
ikuutaqtuq	drills
ikuutautit	drill bits
ila	relative; part; piece
ilaani	sometimes
ilaanilu/ilaanittauq	see you again sometime
ilaaqtuqtaa/ilaaqtaa	patches it; adds a piece to it
ilagiik	two related people
ilainnunngaqtaa	puts him/her/it with the others
ilakhaq	a usable piece or part
ilaktut (*also* illaktut)	are tangled
ilakuq *(pl. ilakuit) (also* amikuq)	leftover
ilannaq	friend
ilannariik	two friends
ilarahuktuq (*also* ilirahuktuq) (*see* ilirahuuq)	is intimidated
ilaranaittuq (*also* iliranaittuq)	is kind; is nice; is friendly
ilaranaqtuq (*also* iliranaqtuq)	is intimidating; is unkind
ilaruhiq	relative; relation
ilaruhirijaa (*also* ilagijaa)	is related to him/her/it; is his/her/its relation
ilaun/ilaut/ilauti	a scoop to remove ice from a fishing hole
ilauqtuq	scoops the ice from a fishing hole
ilgaak/ilgak	eyeglasses
iliarjuk	orphan; abandoned child
iliffi	you (plural)
ilihaijaa (*see* ilihautijaa)	teaches it
ilihaiji	teacher
ilihaijuq	teaches
ilihaqtaa	learns it

ilihaqtuq	learns
iliharvigijaa	learns from him/her/it; it is his/her school
iliharvik (*also* sikuurvik)	school
ilihautijaa (*see* ilihaijaa)	teaches him/her/it
ilihimajara	I know him/her/it; I am familiar with him/her/it
ilihimajuq	knows; knows how
ilihimanngittuq	does not know (how); is not familiar with...
ilihimmariktuq	learns fast; is intelligent
ilijaa	places it; puts it down
ilikkuuqtuq (*also* ilikkuurujuq)	is independent
ilikkuurujuktuq	is consistently independent
ilikkuurujuq (*also* ilikkuuqtuq)	is independent
ilingaijaqtuq	making oneself look good
ilingaittuq	pitiful looking
ilingajuq	is poor
ilingnik	you (as the object of a sentence); by yourself; on your own
ilipiruq	inner slipper
iliptik	the two of you
iliqpik (*also* iliuqpik)	storage place; shelf; drawer
ilirahuktuq (*also* ilarahuktuq) (*see* ilirahuuq)	is intimidated
ilirahuuq (*see* ilarahuktuq, ilirahuktuq)	always intimidated or scared; hesitant to look at people
iliranaittuq (*also* ilaranaittuq)	is kind; is nice; is friendly
iliranaqtuq (*also* ilaranaqtuq)	is intimidating; is unkind
ilitarijaa	recognizes him/her/it
ilitarnaqtuq	looks familiar; can be recognized; is recognizable
iliuqpik (*also* iliqpik)	shelf; storage place; drawer
illaijut/illaijun/illaijaut	a comb

illaktut (*also* ilaktut)	are tangled
illaujaq	candle ice
illuktuq	is snowblind
illuut/illuutik	slingshot
ilu (*see* patuk)	frost formed inside the house; the interior
ilua	the inside
iluani	inside of it
iluittuq	is whole; is complete
ilukittuq	can contain only a small quantity
iluliittuq	has nothing inside
ilulilik	has something inside
ilulliik	long underwear; long johns; underclothing (worn under pants)
ilulliq	innermost
ilumuuqtuq (*see* iqunngittuq)	it is the truth
ilunngunaqtuq (*also* ilun'ngunaqtuq)	is cute
ilun'ngunaqtuq (*also* ilunngunaqtuq)	is cute
ilupaaq	undershirt; inner parka with fur towards body
ilutujuq	can hold a lot; can contain a lot
iluviqhivik	graveyard
iluviq (d. *iluviik*, pl. *iluvrit*)	grave
iluviqtaa	buries him/her/it (a body)
iluvirvik	casket
iluvruaq	T-shirt
ilvit	you (singular)
imaa (*see* imaatun)	like this; this is how; in this way; do it this way
imaaqtuq	falls into water
imaatun (*see* imaa)	like this; this way

INUINNAQTUN TO ENGLISH

imaiqtaa	empties it
imaiqtittuq	tide is out; low tide
imaiqtuq	has been emptied
imaittuq	is empty; is like this; thing (unspecified)
imani	some time ago
imannaaqtuq (see qinngijuq, niaqulrujuq)	says no
imannaq (see i'; ih [slang])	no
imaq	water
imariktuq	good fresh water
Imaruqtirvia	June (it turns to water)
imaruqtuq	has turned to water; has melted (ice or snow)
imiaqtuq (see imiarjijuq)	echoes
imiarjijuq (see imiaqtuq)	echoes once
imiarjiraqtuq	echoes more than once
imingajuq	is drunk
imiq	drinkable (potable) water
imiqtaa	drinks it
imiqtaqti	water delivery person
imiqtaqtuq	fetches water
imiqtaun/imiqtaut/imiqtauti	water truck
imiqtuq (also -tuq-, niuqqaqtuq, niuqhijuq)	drinks
imiraq	broth
imiraqtuun (see urviujaq)	bowl
imiruktuq (see immiqijuq)	is thirsty
imitqutailaq	Arctic tern
immaqaak (also ahu)	maybe; probably
immiqijuq (see imiruktuq)	is thirsty/playing with water
immiqtaa	fills it
immitqiktaa	refills it

immittuq	drowns
immiugaq	homebrew
immiuqtuq	melts ice or snow to make water; makes homebrew
imnaiq	sheep (cliff-dweller)
imnaq	cliff
imngun/imngut/imngum/ imngut	drinking glass
imuniin/imuniit	wrinkles (on face)
ingattaqtuq	is getting worse
ingilraan/-raat	a long time ago; formerly
ingittuq	sits down
ingiuqtuq (*see atuqtuq, huqullaaqtuq*)	sings a drum dance song
ingmiqtuq	hums
ingnak (*also ingnikhaq*)	flintstone
ingnikhaq (*also ingnak*)	flintstone
ingniq (*see auma*)	fire/ember
ingniquhiqiji	mechanic
ingniqun/ingniqut/ingniquti	motor
ingniqutilik	motorboat
ingnirvik	stove
ingutaaqtuq	moves about; is agitated
ini	place; space
inikhaittuq	there is no place; there is no space; there is no room
inikhaqaqtuq	there is space; there is room; there is a place
inikhaqqukittuq	there is little room
inikhaqquqtujuq (*also* inituiuq) (*see* nirutujuq)	there is lots of room; there is enough space
ininikhijuq	makes room for someone/ something
ininiktaa	makes room for him/her/it

iniqtuq

iniqtuq	finishes; is finished; is ready; is complete
inirnikhaaq/inutuqaq	Elder
inirniq	adult
iniruajuq (*also*** inituqtuq)**	follows a human-made trail
init	sled trail; human-made trail
initujuq (*also*** inikhaqquqtujuq)**	there is a lot of room; there is a lot of space
inituqtuq (*also*** iniruajuq)**	follows a human-made trail
initurliq (*see*** tangmaarvik)**	old camp site
innaqtuq	goes to bed; is lying in bed
in'ngaqtuq	leaks
in'ngutaq/irngutaq	grandchild
inuaqtaa (*see*** tuqutaa)**	murdered him/her
inuaqtaujuq (*see*** tuqutaujuq)**	was murdered
inuaqtuq (*see*** tuquttijuq)**	kills someone; is killed by someone
inuarullik	dwarf; Inuit mythical character
inugaq (*pl.*** *inukkat*)**	toe; finger
inugiaktuq	it is full; there are lots of people
inugiaktut (*see*** amigaittut, amihut)**	there are many; they are numerous
inuhaaq	newborn
inuilaq	uninhabited place; place where nobody lives
Inuinnaq	a real Inuk; an Inuit person
Inuinnaqtun	in an Inuit way; like an Inuinnaq; the language of the Inuinnait
inuittuq	there is nobody there
inuk	person; human being
inukhiarijaa (*see*** paaqtaa)**	expecting to meet him/her/it
inukhijuq	meets someone by chance
inukhuk	rock cairn; land marker

inukpagjuaq/inukpak	giant; Tunniq
inutquaq	old man
inuuhuktuq	teenaged boy
inuujaq	doll
inuujuq	is alive; is a person
inuuqati (*see* **aippaq**)	person of the same age; partner; spouse
inuuqatigijaa	accompanies him/her; is his/her spouse; lives with him/her
ipigaun	lever
ipiiqtuq	is dull; is no longer sharp; became loose
ipijuq	suffocates; smothers
ipikhaijuq	sharpens something
ipikhaqtaa	sharpens it
ipikharniq	sharp edge of knife, axe; cutting edge of a knife, axe
ipikhaun	sharpener
ipiktuq	is sharp
ipiqtuq	is tied (with a rope or chain)
ipirakhat (*see* **kanguujaq**)	mantle for a lamp; Arctic cotton used as a wick in traditional lamp (qulliq)
ipiraq	wick
ipirautik	waterproof kamik; hip waders
ipiutaq	chain or rope to tie dogs or boats
ippakhaani/ikpakhaani	day before yesterday
ippakhaq/ikpakhaq	yesterday
ippakhaq ublaami/ikpakhaq ublaami	yesterday morning
ippakhaq x-munngarman/ ikpakhaq x-munngarman	yesterday at _ o'clock
iptiiqtuq	has no more flavour
iptiittuq	has no flavour

ipu	handle
ipualik (*also* ipulik) (*see* hiratittit; hiqanakhiut/ hiqanakhiun/hiqanakhiuti; haqanakhiut)	pot or pan with a handle
ipulvik (*also* paurvik)	oarlock
ipummingajuq	keeps his/her/its mouth closed
ipummiqtuq	closes his/her/its mouth
iqalgagiaq (*also* iqilgagiaq)	Sabine's gull
iqalliaqtuq	is going fishing
iqalliqijut	get lots of fish
iqaluk	fish of the salmonid family (char, trout, etc.)
iqalukhiun/iqalukhiut (*see* iqqaqhaut)	fishing rod
iqalukhiuqtuq	is fishing
iqalukpik	Arctic char
iqaluktuq	catches a fish
Iqaluktuuttiaq	good fishing place (Cambridge Bay)
iqaluqarvik (*also* iqaluut)	container to hold fish
iqaluut (*also* iqaluqarvik)	container to hold fish
iqhigijaa (*see* kappiagijaa)	is frightened by him/her/it; is afraid of him/her/it; is scared of him/her/it
iqhijuq (*see* kappiahuktuq)	is scared; is frightened; is afraid
iqhinaqtuq (*see* kappianaqtuq)	is scary; is frightening
iqhiqpak	molar (back tooth)
iqiahuktuq	is lazy
iqiahuujuq	is habitually lazy
iqilgagiag (*also* iqalgagiaq)	Sabine's gull
iqingajuq	has curly hair; is in a kneeling position
iqitaa	hugs him/her/it

iqitquq	little finger
iqqakuuq	garbage
iqqakuuqti	garbage collector
iqqakuurun/iqqakuurut/ iqqakuuruti	garbage truck
iqqakuurvik	garbage can/bin
iqqanaiqtuq (*also* itqanaiqtuq)	is ready
iqqaqhaut (*see* iqalukhiun)	fishing rod
iqqaqtuq	throws something
iqquk *(d. iqquuk)* (*see* nuluq)	buttock; heart in a deck of cards
iqquuk	buttocks; that's a lie!
iqujuq (*see* haglujuq)	cheats; lies; does not tell the truth
iqunngittuq	he/she is not lying
iqutujuq (*see* haglujuq)	always cheats; always lies
iquutikhaq	toilet paper
irijuq (*see* qalingujuq)	shedding its fur
irinahuktuq	rushes around; is in a hurry
iritaqtuq	plucks a bird
irmiun/irmiut/irmiuti	soap; detergent
irngutaq/in'ngutaq	grandchild
irnikhaq	stepson
irniq	son
irnituaq	only son
itigak	foot
itijuq	is deep
itiktaqtuq	has diarrhea
itimak	palm of hand
itingmigaqtuq	playing soccer
itingmiktaa	kicks him/her/it
itiq	anus

itiqhaq *(d. iqharlurut)*	dimple
itiqtuq	enters; comes in
itiruk	bring it inside
itiruq/itirurni	strong urine
itivjaaq	portage
itivjaaqtuq *(see ikaaqtuq)*	crosses over; portages
itkiq	gum (of the mouth)
itqakhaijuq *(also itqaqhaqtuq)*	tries to remember
itqanaijaqtuq	gets ready
itqanaiqtuq *(also iqqanaiqtuq)*	is ready
itqaqhaqtuq *(also itqakhaijuq)*	tries to remember
itqaqtaa	remembers him/her/it
itqaqtuq	remembers
Itqiliq	a First Nations person; a Dene person
itqiq	louse egg; nit
itqujaq	sea urchin
itquqtuq	sits on his/her/its eggs; guesses it
ittuaqtuq	looks in
ittuq	is here
ituk	milk
iukkaqtuq *(also ijukkaqtuq)*	falls
ivajuq	nests; nurses its young
ivalu	sinew (for sewing)
ivalukhaq	thread
ivalukhaun	spool for thread
ivgun/ivgut/ivguti	napkin; wiper; rag; cloth for wiping
iviangiilitaq	brassiere
iviangiq *(d. iviangik)*	breast
ivik *(pl. ivgit)*	blade of grass
ivitaaruq	spawning char

iviurnauti	special friend; someone you really care about; a sweetheart
ivjaqun/ivjaqut/ivjaquti (*also* ivjarun)	scarf wrapped around face; dog muzzle; surgical mask
ivjaruhiqtaa	puts a scarf around someone's face; puts on a surgical mask; muzzles it
ivjaruhiqtuqtaa	wraps a scarf around it (someone's face, dog's muzzle); is muzzling it
ivjarun/ivjarut/ivjaruti (*also* ivjaqun)	scarf wrapped around face; surgical mask; dog muzzle
ivjuhiliqtaa	makes it thicker
ivjuhiliqtuq	thickens by itself
ivjujuq	is thick
ivujuq/ivuuqtuq	the ice is piled up

juus/juusi	juice

kaaktuq	is hungry
kaapi/kaaffi	coffee
kaapiliurut (*also* kaapiliut)	coffee pot

kaapiliut (*also* kaapiliurut)	coffee pot
kaavjiq	tip of parka hood
kablaq	bearberry
kablaqutit	bearberry/crowberry leaves (for tea)
kahakaffuktaa	barely touches him/her/it; grazes him/her/it
kahaktaa	touches him/her/it
kaiffan'nguqtuq	dizzy from spinning around
kaimalluriktuq	circle
kaipiktidjutijuk/ kaiffiqtidjutijuk/ kaiffiktidjutijuk/ kaiffittidjutijuk	they (two) miss each other by going in different directions, or at different times
kaiptaq	spinning top
kaivaluaqtuq	spins around; goes around something
kaivittuq	spins; swirls
kaivjaqtaa (*also* qiputiqtaa, qipitiqtaa)	coils it; spins it around something
kajumiittuq	is slow
kajumiktuq	is fast
kajuqtuq (*see* marlungajuq)	red fox; brown
kakaktuq	carries something on his/her/its shoulders
kakautaq	tumpline
kakilahaaq	the feeling of having pins and needles
kakilahaijuq	gets pins and needles in a limb
kakilahak	smelt (fish)
kakillarnaq	thorn
kakiniq	facial tattoo
kakivak (*see* nuijaaqpak)	leister; three-pronged fishing spear

kakkiijaun/kakkiijaut/ kakkiijauti	tissue; kleenex
kakkiktuq	blows his/her/its nose
kakkiliqtaqtuq (*see* **niurmiktuq)**	sniffles
kakkiviaq	upper lip and groove under nose
kalluguqtuq (*also* **kalluktuq)**	there is thunder; it is thundering
kalluk	thunder
kalluktuq (*also* **kalluguqtuq)**	it is thundering; there is thunder
kallulaqijuq	it is starting to thunder
kamiijaqtuq	takes his/her/its boots or shoes off
**kamik *(*d. *kammak,* pl. *kamngit)*	boot; shoe
kamiktuq	has his/her/its boots or shoes on
kamiktuqtuq	puts his/her/its boots or shoes on
kanajuq	sculpin; bullhead (type of small fish)
kanajuraq	small sculpin; small bullhead (type of small fish)
kanangnaq	north wind
kanangnaqtuq	the wind is blowing from the north
kangiqhihurnaqtuq (*see* **uingairnaqtuq)**	is easy to understand (of language, manner of speech)
kangiqhijaa (*also* **uingaiqtaa)**	understands him/her/it
kangiqhilimaittuq (*also* **kangiqhimanngittuq) (***see* **uingajuq)**	cannot understand
kangiqhimanngittuq (*also* **kangiqhilimaittuq) (***see* **uingajuq)**	cannot understand
kangiqhuk	bay
kanguq	snow goose
kanguujaq (*see* **ipirakhat)**	Arctic cotton (resembles snow goose)

kanivaun/kanivaut/kanivauti	diaphragm in the chest cavity
kanna	that one down there
kan'nguhuktuq	is shy
kannujaq	copper
kapihijuq	stabs someone/something
kapihik	fish scale
kapihilik	whitefish; a fish that has scales
kapiittuq	a very knowledgeable person
kapijaa	gives him/her/it an injection; stabs him/her/it
kapijuq	stabs himself/herself/itself; gives himself/herself an injection
kapittuq (*also* hukangajuq)	tight clothing
kappiagijaa (*see* iqhigijaa)	is afraid of him/her/it
kappiahuktuq (*see* iqhijuq)	is in distress; is alarmed; is scared; is afraid
kappianaqtuq (*see* iqhinaqtuq)	is distressing; is alarming; is scary; is frightening
kapuittuq	a learner
kapuraun/kapuraut/kapurauti	fork
kapuun/kapuut/kapuuti	harpoon; spear; injection needle; spade in deck of cards
kataktaa	drops him/her/it
katilvik (*also* katimavik)	meeting place; gathering place
katimajut	are having a meeting; are together
katimavik (*also* katilvik)	meeting place; gathering place
katitirijuq	gathers something
katittait	gathered them
katittut	are gathered/are together
kattuaq	bicep
katuktuq	beats the drum
katuun/katuut/katuuti	stick for beating a drum; drumstick

kaugvik	anvil; stone on which to crack bones
kautaujaq	hammer
kauttuaq	pocket
kauttuarminunngaqtaa	puts it in his/her own pocket
kauttuarmiutarijaa	keeps it in his/her/its own pocket
kia	whose
kiahik *(d. kiattik)*	shoulder blade
kiahirutilik	cross fox
kialaqijuq/qaajurnaiqtuq/ kiaruqtuq	the weather is warm
kidjak	fever
kidjaktuq	has a fever
kidjalaqijuq	developed a fever
kigiaq	beaver
kigiqtuq	it (animal) gnaws (on skins or clothing)
kiglingani	at its edge; on his/her/its border; on his/her/its boundary
kigliq	end; border; boundary
kiglukkuuqtuq	goes the wrong way
kiguhiqiji *(also kigutiliqiji)*	dentist
kiguhiqijuq	brushes or works on his/her/its teeth
kiguhiqqun/kiguhiqqut/ kiguhiqquti	dental instrument; toothbrush
kigulliuqtuq	has a toothache
kigun/kigut/kiguti *(pl. kigutit)*	tooth
kigutaijaqtaa	pulls out his/her/its tooth
kigutaiqtuq	has no more teeth
kigutangirnaq (also kigutigingnaq)	blueberry
kigutigikhaqtuq	brushes his/her/its teeth

kigutigikhaun/kigutigikhaut/kigutigikhauti ....

kigutigikhaun/kigutigikhaut/ kigutigikhauti	toothpaste
kigutigingnaq (*also* **kigutangirnaq)**	blueberry
kigutiliqiji (*also* **kiguhiqiji)**	dentist
kihadjariktuq	(a boat) is well anchored
kihaq	anchor
kihaqtuq	(a boat) is anchored
kihiani (*also* **kihimi)**	only him/her/it; but
kihimi (*also* **kihiani)**	only him/her/it; but
kihimmiuqtuq	went/travelling by himself; is by himself
kihimngiuqtuq	stays alone
kihimngiurumajuq	wants to be alone
kihittijuq (*also* **kihittitirijuq)**	counts
kihittitirijuq (*also* **kihittijuq)**	counts
kii (*see* **kiluuttaq)**	key
kiihijuq	bites someone/something
kiijaa	bites him/her/it
kiijuq	crimping ugjuk soles with his/her teeth
kiiliqtaa (*also* **kiluuttaqtaa)**	locks it
kiilliq	the farthest out at sea/farthest one
kiinaa	ulu/knive/axe blade
kiinannguaq	mask
kiinaq (*also* **akuliak/akuliaq) (***see* **qauq)**	face; forehead
kijuaqtuqtuq	aims at something with a gun (or other object)
kikhugvik	fireplace (made with rocks)
kikhuutit (*see* **ikhun)**	Arctic heather used to start fire
kikiak	nail (for building)
kikiaktaa	nails it

kikiaktuqtaa	nails it in several places
kikkariktuq	square
kikturiaq	mosquito
kikturiijaun/kikturiijaut/ kikturiijauti	bug repellent
kikturiilitaq	mosquito net
kilgavik	peregrine falcon
kilgavikpak	gyrfalcon
kiliqtaa	cuts him/her/it
kiliqtuq	cuts himself/herself/itself
killaijaijuq	mends a seam
killaijaqtaa	mends it (a seam)
kiluaqtuq	becomes unstitched
kiluuttaq (*see* kii)	latch; lock
kiluuttaqtaa (*also* kiiliqtaa)	locks it
kimik (*also* kinamik)	whom
kimik atiqaqqit (*see* kinauvit, kina atqin)	what's your name
kina (d. *kitkuk,* pl. *kitkut*)	who
kina atqin (*also* kinauvit, kimik atiqaqqit)	what's your name
kinamik (*also* kimik)	whom
kinauvit (*also* kina atqin, kimik atiqaqqit)	what's your name
kingmautik (*see* tiggutik)	pliers
kingmiktaq	Russian dance (kicking one's heels)
kingmingnaq	cranberry
kingmitquq	heel
kinguani	in the rear part of...; at the end of....
kingulliq	the last one; rear
kingullirmi	the last time

INUINNAQTUN TO ENGLISH

kingumun/kingumut

|---|---|
kingumun/kingumut (*see* utimun/utimut)	backwards
kinguniq	empty gun shell
kinguq	krill (resembles a small shrimp)
kinittijuq	traditional form of toilet training
kinnguqtaa/kinnguijaa	misses him/her/it; wishes him/her/it back
kipaqati (*also* nanngutiqati)	teasing partner
kipaqatigiiktuk (*also* nanngutiqatigiiktuk)	they (two) tease each other
kipataa	teases him/her/it; is kidding him/her/it
kipattijuq	teases someone; is kidding someone
kipihimajuq	has been cut off; is severed
kipijaa	cuts it
kipijuq	cuts something
kipkaq	bone for gnawing or picking
kipkaqtaa	gnaws it; picks at it; chews on it
kipkaqtuq	gnaws (human)
kipkariktuq	bone with meat and fat, good for gnawing
kitautiqtuq	passes at a distance; stays in the offing
kitauttuq	went/passed by (travelling on ice or water)
kitkuk (*see* kina)	which two?
kitkut (*see* kina)	who (more than two people)
kiujaa	answers him/her/it
kiujuq	answers
kivanmun/kivanmut	eastward
kivgaluk	muskrat
kivgaq	servant; maid; domestic helper

kivgaqtuqtuq	works as a servant/maid; does domestic work for someone
kivijuq	sinks
kiviktaa	lifts him/her/it up
kivjaqtaa	cuts it with scissors
kivjautik	scissors
kivvin/kivvit/kivviti (*see*** titqaun)**	weight for a fishnet
kuapigaq (pl. *kuapikkat***)(***see*** qimirluk)**	vertebra
kuapikkat (sing. *kuapigaq***)(***also*** qimirluk)**	vertebrae; backbone; spinal column; spine
kublu	thumb
kuhiqtaqtuq	drips repeatedly
kuhiqtuq	drips
kuhirniq (*also*** hikuarniq, qurlurniq)**	icicle; a stain where something has dripped
kuhirnirit	puddles made by something dripping
kujaktuq	has sex
kukialuk	a cook
kukiijaut/kukiijautik	nail clipper
kukik	fingernail; toenail; claw; talon
kukiktaa (*also*** tigliktaa)**	steals it
kukiktuq (*also*** tigliktuq)**	steals
kukiujuq (*see*** niqiliuqtuq)**	cooks
kukuktuq	is itchy
kukukuulaq	Coca-Cola; soft drink
kukuulaaqtuq/-t (*also*** tiitaqtut)**	boisterous/noisy
kulavak	female caribou (cow)
kumak	louse
kumiktuq	scratches an itch
kuniktaa	kisses him/her/it

kuniktuq	kisses
kuttuq	chewing gum
kuugaq	river
kuugarjuk (*also* kuutiruq)	creek
kuummiujaaqtuq/ kummiuhaaqtuq	whistles
kuungajuq	his/her/its feet are turned in
kuutiruq (*also* kuugarjuk)	creek
kuvijaa	spills it; pours it out
kuvijuq/kuvihijuq	spills; runs over; overflows
kuvjaq	fishnet
kuvjaqhuqtuq	checks a fishnet
kuvjaqtaa	catches it with a fishnet
kuvjaqtuqtuq (*also* kuvjiqtuq, kuvjiqhijuq)	sets a fishnet
kuvjin	netting needle (to repair fishnets)
kuvjiqhijuq (*see* kuvjaqtuqtuq, kuvjiqtuq)	sets a fishnet
kuvjiqtuq (*see* kuvjaqtuqtuq, kuvjiqhijuq)	sets a fishnet

maamak (*also* amaamak)	mother
maamakhaq (*also* amaamakhaq, arnakhaq)	stepmother
maamaktuq (*also* amaamaktuq)	nurses; sucks milk
maamaun/maamaut/maamauti (*also* amaamaun)	baby bottle

madjaaqtuq	dark spot in the distance
mahak	melting snow
mahakhiqtuq	thawing it out
mahaktiqtuq	it is melting
mahaktuq	it melted; snow is melting
mahik	gills of a fish
mahuk/mahu	edible root
majuaqtuq (*also* **majuraqtuq)**	climbs up; goes uphill; goes upriver
majuqqaq	side of a mountain
majuraqtuq (*also* **majuaqtuq)**	climbs up; goes uphill; goes upriver
majurautaq/majuraun (*see* **tungmiqqat)**	ladder
makanngittuq	misses the target when shooting
makaqhuqtuq	is good at shooting; is good at hitting the target
makaqtaa	shoots it/him/her; gets it by shooting
makitaa	sets it upright; stands it up
makittuq	gets up from a prone or sitting position; stands up from a prone or sitting position
makkaq	diaper
makpiraaq (*see* **qun'ngiaq)**	book; magazine
makpiraaqarvik (*also* **taiguaqarvik)**	library
makpiraq	page
makpiraqtuq	turns the page
maktak/maktaaq	muktuk (edible part of whale skin; not blubber)
malik	wave
maliktaa	follows behind him/her/it
maliriq (*see* **qaqhauq, tuullik)**	Arctic loon

mallaujuq	follows behind
malliqtuq	there are waves
malriak (*also* malrik)	twins
malrijuq	has twins
malrik (*also* malriak)	twins
malruiqtaqtut	are going two at a time
malruiqtuqtuq	does it twice
malruk/malruuk	two
malrunnguqtait	divides them into two piles, groups
malruraaqtuq	catches, gets two of something
mamaqhungnittuq	smells good (of food)
mamaqtuq	is delicious; tastes good; smells good
mamarijaa	likes the taste/smell of it
mamiahujuittuq	never gets angry; never loses his/her temper; is always patient
mamiahuktuq	is disgruntled; is annoyed; is impatient
mamianaq	sorry
mamittuq	is cured; heals
maniilaq	rough ice
maniillat	patches of rough ice
manik	money
maniliqiji	treasurer; accountant
maniqautit	funding sources
maniqautit ukiunga	fiscal year
manittuq	receiving retaliation after being mean or irritating for a long time; he was asking for it
mannik (pl. *manniit*)	egg
manniliuqtuq	lays an egg
maqijuq	flows; leaks

maraaqtuq	whimpers (of dogs); howls with pain
marluk	mud
marlungajuq (*see* **kajuqtuq**)	brown (resembles mud)
mauligaqujaanga	asking to look for seal breathing holes under the snow before seal hunting
mauliqtuq (*see* **nippaqtuq, atiqtuq**)	looking for seal breathing hole under the snow
mihiktuq	jumps in the air; jumps over
mihuktuq	soaked with liquid
mihuraq/mihuraaq	aged blubber (used to dip food in)
mikhaanun	towards
mikhijuq	shrinks; gets smaller
mikigaq	raw meat; raw fish
mikijuq (*also* **-nnuaq, -arjuk**)	is small
mikiliraq	ring finger
mikilirarmiaq	ring
mikitqijaq	smaller one
mikkirun	bait on a hook
millalauqtuq (*also* **mittaqtuqtuq**)	lands slowly
milugiaq	blackfly; sucker fish
milukaqtuq	sucks
milukattak	wasp
milvik	airstrip; landing strip, place to land
mimiq	side of buttock
minguk	paint (like a fresh layer of powder snow)
minguktaa	paints it
mingulilaqijuq	there is blowing powder snow
minguliq	falling powder snow
minguliqhijuq	paints

minguliqtuq	it is snowing wet snow
minguliruqtuq	powder snow is falling
minihitaq	minister
minilaqijuq	drizzles
miniq	drizzle; very light rain
minittailijaa	puts it aside for someone
mipku	dry meat
miqhuqtaa	sews it; stitches him/her/it up
miqhuqtitaq	sewing machine
miqhuqtuq	sews
miriaqtuq	vomits
mirraaq	newborn baby
mitiinnaq	"It's only a female eider duck" (expression)
mitiq (*see*** hurluqtuuq)**	king eider duck (female)
mitquiqhijuq	scrapes hair or fur off a hide
mitquiqtaa	scrapes the hair or fur off it (a hide)
mitquiqtuq	has no more hair, fur, feathers; has shed all its hair, fur, feathers
mitqukittuq	has short hair
mitqun/mitqut/mitquti	sewing needle
mitquq *(pl. mitquit)* (*see*** nujaq, tingiq, huluk)**	fur; human body hair; feather
mittaqtuqtuq (*also*** millalauqtuq)**	lands slowly
mittarvik	airport
mittuq	bird or plane lands
muluilitaq	cap under lid of a baby bottle to prevent leaking; fur nipple protector (for breastfeeding dogs, to prevent freezing)
munaqhi	nurse
muqpak	ball

muqpaujaq	flour; bannock; bread (resembles a ball)
murruuqtuq	howling

naalaktuq	listens
naalaun/naalaut/naalauti	radio
naammadjavutit *(d.* ***naammadjvutik,*** **pl.** ***naammadjavuhi)***	stay well; take care
naammaktuq	is enough; is sufficient; is all right; is fine
naarliuqtuq *(also* **aqiarurliuqtuq, aqiarurliqtuq, nadjagliqtuq)**	has a stomach ache
nadjagliqtuq *(also* **aqiarurliuqtuq, aqiarurliqtuq, naarliuqtuq)**	has a stomach ache
nadjak *(see* **aqiaruq)**	belly
nagjuk	antler; horn
nagjungmiktaa	gores him/her/it with antlers or horns; hits him/her/it with antlers or horns
nagligijaa	pities him/her/it
naglingnaqtuq	is pitiful
nagluqitaqtuq	juggles
nahaq *(see* **naharaq)**	parka hood; hat
naharaq *(see* **nahaq, titqiaq)**	hat; cap
nahaullik	Lapland longspur
naimajuq	smells something

naittuq	is short
najak	younger sister of a male
najakhaq	younger stepsister of a male
najuqtaa	stays with him/her/it; lives with him/her/it
nakahuk	bladder
nakahungnaq	calf of a leg
nakin/nakit	from where
nakin pijat	where did you get it from
nakit qaivit	where did you come from
nakkaqtuq	falls through (ice, floor, etc.)
nakujuq	cross-eyed
nakuugijaa	likes him/her/it
nakuugilluanngitaa	does not like him/her/it very much
nakuuginngitaa	does not like him/her/it
nakuujuq	is good
nakuunngittuq	is bad
nalariaq	horizontal ridgepole of tent
nalaumajuq	fits just right; fits well
naliak	which one (of two)
naliat	which one (of many)
nalujaa	does not know him/her/it; cannot figure it out; finds it confusing
nalujuq	confused; cannot figure it out; does not know what to do
naluktuq	wades into water
nalunaqtuq (*also* **naunaqtuq**)	is difficult; is hard to understand
naluujaqtuq	swims
naluujauti	bathing suit; swimsuit
nalvaaqhiuqtuq	in search of something
nalvaaqtaa	finds it by chance

nangiaqtuittuq/ nangiaqtujuittuq	brave; not scared of going in boats, planes, or on ice
nangiaqtuq	is afraid to go on ice, or in a boat or plane; is afraid of falling or falling through
nangiarnaqtuq	is dangerous (of ice, water, boat, plane)
nangiqtuq	stands up
nangirvigijaa	stands on it
nangmaktaq	backpack; packsack
nangmaktuq	packs something on the back; carries something on the back
nangmautaq	strap around the chest for securing a backpack
nangutaa	teases him/her/it; picks on him/her/it
nani	where; in what place; at what place; on what
nanihijuq	found it; found something
nanijaa	finds him/her/it
naniriaq	leghold trap
naniriaqturvik	trapline
naniruaqtuq	searching with the flashlight lit
naniruun/naniruut/naniruuti	flashlight
nanngudjijuq (*also* nannguttijuq)	teases someone; picks on someone
nanngutiqati (*also* kipaqati)	teasing partner
nanngutiqatigiiktuk (*also* kipaqatigiiktuk)	they (two) tease each other
nannguttijuq (*also* nanngudjijuq)	teases someone; picks on someone
nanuaq	young polar bear; polar bear cub
nanuq	polar bear
nanuqtuq	gets a polar bear
napaaqtuq	stands upright; is upright; tree

napajuq ....

napajuq	stands upright, set up (tent)
napariaq	upright tent pole
napu	crosspiece on a sled
napuliut	rope for tying crosspieces of a sled
naqhaq	valley
naqittuq	is flat; is low
naqujaqtuq	has a bad taste; smells bad; is sour
narlungajuq	goes in a straight line
natiq	floor
natirluit	patches of dirt on bottom of lake, sea
natirnaq	flat land; a plain
natiruvik	drifting snow
natiruvilaqijuq	snow blowing along a surface
natiruvilaqutijuq	dust or snow is blowing behind a moving vehicle
natquq	bullet tip; arrowhead
nattiaq	seal pup
nattiq	seal
nattiqtuq	gets a seal
naujaq	glaucous gull
nauk	where
nauk taimna	where is he/she/it
naulaq	harpoon head
nauligaq	harpoon for throwing
nauliktaa	harpoons it
naunaipkuhiqtaa (*also* **naunaitkuhiqtaa**)	marks it for recognition
naunaipkutaq (*also* **naunaitkutaq**)	marker for recognition or identification
naunaitkuhiqtaa (*also* **naunaipkuhiqtaa**)	marks it for recognition

naunaitkutaq (*also* naunaipkutaq)	marker for recognition or identification
naunaqquq (*see* huukiaq)	I do not know; I do not know why
naunaqtuq (*also* nalunaqtuq)	is difficult or impossible to understand
nauttiaq	plant; flower
navikhimajuq	is broken
naviktaa	breaks it
naviktuq	breaks
navvaq	piece of a broken object
niaqulrujuq (*see* imannaaqtuq, qinngijuq)	says no; shakes his head indicating no
niaqun'ngujuq (*also* niaqurliuqtuq)	has a headache
niaqurliuqtuq (*also* niaqun'ngujuq)	has a headache
niaqurluktuq	has something wrong in the head (headache, brain damage, mental disability)
nibliqtuq	says something
nigaq	snare
nigaqtaa	catches it in a snare
nigaqtuq	snares something
nigaqtuqtuq	uses snares
nigiq	east wind
nigiqtuq	wind is blowing from the east
nigituraqtuq	hiccoughs; has the hiccups
niglaqhiqtuq	letting something hot cool off
niglaqtiqtuq	becomes cold (weather)
niglaqtuq	becomes cold
nikhaaktuq	burps
nikhik	fishing hook
nikhiktaa	catches it with a hook
nikpaqtuq (*also* nippaqtuq)	waits at a seal's breathing hole

nikpaqujaanga

nikpaqujaanga	was told to wait at a seal's breathing hole
niliqtuq	farts
ningahuktuq	is angry
ningaqtut	they fight each other
ningauk	son-in-law; brother-in-law
nipalliqtuq	it is raining
nipaluk	rain
nipi	voice; sound; noise
nipikhaun/nipikhaut/ nipikhauti	recording tape; blank cassette tape; blank CD
nipiliun/nipiliut/nipiliuti (*also* nipiliurun)	tape recorder; audio recorder
nipiliuqtuq	tape records; records audio
nipiliurun/nipiliurut/ nipiliuruti (*also* nipiliun)	tape recorder; audio recorder
nipin'ngajuq	sticks to something; is stuck to something; sticky tape
nipitirun/nipitirut/nipitiruti	glue
nipitqaqtaun/nipitqaqtaut/ nipitqaqtauti	magnet
nipitqaqtuq	sticky
nipittaaqtuq	is easy to stick; sticks easily
nipittuq	sticks to something
nippaqtuq (*also* nikpaqtuq)	waits at a seal's breathing hole
niqait	gums of the mouth
niqi	food; meat
niqikhaqtaa	gets him/her/it something to eat
niqiliqijuq	butchering wildlife
Niqiliqivik	August
niqiliuqtuq (*see* kukiujuq)	makes food to eat; cooks; prepares food
nirijaa (*also* -tuq-)	eats it
nirijuq (*also* -tuq-)	eats

niriniaqtuq	grazes; will eat
niripkaqtaa	feeds him/her/it
nirjun/nirjut/nirjuti (*also* anngun)	game animal
nirlirnaq	black brant
nirlivik	white-fronted goose
nirrit (pl. *nirritit*)	table knife; eating utensil
nirumiktuq	is soft and warm
nirutujuq	spacious
niu	leg; skin of a caribou leg
niudjijuq	allows him/her/it to disembark; lets him/her/it off of a boat or out of a vehicle
niudjivik (*see* apurvik, tulagvik)	dock; unloading place; a place to disembark; landing place; a place to get off
niujijuq	comes off/out accidentally
niujuq	gets out of a vehicle or boat; disembarks; removes a baby from an amaut
niuqhijuq (*also* imiqtuq, -tuq-, niuqqaqtuq)	sips; takes a sip; drinks
niuqqaqtuq (*also* imiqtuq, -tuq-, niuqhijuq)	drinks
niurmiktuq (*see* kakkiliqtaqtuq)	sniffs; sniffles
niuviqtaa	buys it
niuviqtuq	buys
niuvirvik (*also* situa)	store
niuvvaavik	a shop
nivaktaa	digs him/her/it out
nivinngaqtaa	hangs it up (on a wall)
nivinngarvik	hook; hanger
niviqtuq	falls backwards

niviuqtujuq ....

niviuqtujuq	a timid animal; an animal flying/ running away
niviuqtuq	nesting bird luring prey away from nest or young
niviuvak	fly
niviuvarjuk	small fly
nivjaaqtuq	makes a continuous sound
nuijaaqpak (*see* **kakivak**)	trident; three-pronged fish spear
nuitajuq	shows up; is visible; is showing
nuittiijuq	waits for something/someone to appear
nujaiqtuq	has gone bald; has no more hair
nujaittuq	has no hair; is bald
nujaq *(pl. nujait)* (*see* **mitquq**)	hair on the head
nujarluktuq	has messy hair
nujuaqtujuq	untamed, wild animal
nujuittuq	tame, unafraid animal
nukakhaq	younger stepsister of a female; younger stepbrother of a male
nukaq	younger brother of a male; younger sister of a female
nukariit	siblings
nukatugaq	young male caribou
nukatukkaaq	year-old caribou calf; yearling
nukaun'nguq (*compare* **angajun'nguq, ukuaq**)	sister-in-law (wife of husband's younger brother); brother-in-law (husband of wife's younger sister)
nukigliurniq	has rheumatism
nulaq	crystals of ice (formed on boots, fishnet, sled runners, etc.)
nulialik	married man; has a wife
nuliangiqtuq (*also* **nuliilgaqtuq**)	widower (man who has lost his wife)
nuliaq	wife

nuliilgahuk	bachelor
nuliilgaqtuq (*also* nuliangiqtuq)	widower (man who has lost his wife)
nullauhiqtuq	eats supper
nuluq *(d. **nulluk**) (*see* **iqquk**)*	human buttock
numiktiriji	interpreter; translator (one who turns things over)
numiktirijuq	interprets; translates (turns things over)
numiqtuq/mumiqtuq	dances
nummagiaktuq	gone to the dance
nuna	land
nunaliqun/nunaliqut	pickaxe; spade
nunaturliq	old camping area (where a tent has been pitched)
nunguani	at the end of something about to be finished or depleted
nungulaaq (*also* uqummiaq)	candy
nungulaittumun/ nungulaittumut (*also* taimunga)	forever; without end; endless
nunguqhuqtuq	wears out; is worn out (mainly from rubbing)
nungutaa	finishes it; uses it up; depletes it
nunguttuq	is used up; is depleted; is finished
nunijuq	sweats (animal or person)
nuniq	female seal
nuqhutik	suspenders
nuqitaa	pulls it
nurraittuarjuk	young female caribou
nurrakhaq	stepniece or stepnephew of a woman
nurraq	caribou calf; muskox calf; niece of a woman; nephew of a woman
nutaaq	something new

INUINNAQTUN TO ENGLISH

nutaqqijuq (*also* **utaqqijuq)**	waits; gives birth to a child
nutaraq (d. *nutaqqak,* **pl.** ***nutaqqat)***	child
nutiblik	gray/white hair on a young person; mole
nutqangajuq	stops for a while; is still
nutqaqtuq	stops moving
nuutaa	moves it to another location
nuuttuq	moves to another location
nuvihijuq	threads a needle
nuvijaa	threads it (a needle)
nuvilhaq	jellyfish
nuviqhaaq	knitted or woven item
nuviqhaqtuq	knits; weaves
nuvuja	cloud
nuvujalaqijuq	is cloudy
nuvuk	tip; point

paamnguliaq (*also* **paan'nguliaq)**	seal that crawls far from its breathing hole
paamnguqtuq (*also* **paan'nguqtuq)**	crawls
paan'nguliaq (*also* **paamnguliaq)**	seal that crawls far from its breathing hole
paan'nguqtuq (*also* **paamnguqtuq)**	crawls
paapak (*also* **aappak)**	father
paaq/paa	entrance, doorway

paaqtaa (*see* inukhiarijaa)	comes across him/her/it; meets him/her/it
paatuliiq (*also* quaqhalaarun)	battery
paijuq	stays home while the others are going out
paipak (*also* tuqhuaq)	pipe
paipaut	pipe tobacco
paja (*also* pata)	butter
pajaliqin (*also* pataliqhit, pataliqhin)	butter knife
pakaktuq	making noise while moving stuff
pakkaq	hole; perforation
pallukaqtuq	falls flat on his/her face
palluqtuq	laid down on tummy
palriaqtaa	goes to meet him/her/it
palviittuq	is patient; is kind by nature
palvinaqtuq	is bothersome; is annoying
palvitujuq	is unkind; is impatient by nature
pamialluk	tailbone; coccyx
pamiqhaaq	domestic animal
pamiqhihuktuq	takes good care of
pamirraaqtuq/pamiqhaaqtuq (*see* papiqqiqijuq)	moves/wags its tail (land mammals)
pamiuq (*see* papik, papiruq)	tail of a land mammal
pamiuqtuuq	otter
pangaliktuq	runs on all fours
pangnaarjuk	uncle on father's side
pangniq	bull muskox; bull caribou
panik	daughter
panikhaq	stepdaughter
paniqhidjiqturvik	clothesline
paniqhiivik	drying rack; dryer
paniqhiqtuq	dries; becomes dry

paniqtuq	is dry
panituaq	only daughter
papik (*see* **papiruq, pamiuq**)	tail of a bird
papiqqiqijuq (*see* **pamirraaqtuq**)	moves its tail (of fish, sea mammals)
papiruq (*see* **papik, pamiuq**)	tail of fish
parnaijaqtuq (*also* **hannaijaqtuq; itqanaijaqtuq; upalungaijaqtuq**)	gets ready
pata (*also* **paja**)	butter
pataliqhit/pataliqhin (*also* **pajaliqin**)	butter knife
patau	cooked fish heads
patauliuqtuq	cooks fish heads
patautuqtuq/pataujuq (*see* **qaqquqtuqtuq**)	eats cooked fish heads
patiktaa	pats him/her/it; slaps him/her/it
patiq	bone marrow
patirialaqijuq	has restless legs
patqujaq	candle; wax
pattaaqtaa	pets it; strokes him/her/it; slaps him/her/it
pattitigijaa (*also* **pinahugijaa, -niraq-**)	blames him/her/it; accuses him/her/it
patuk	frost formed inside a house; rime; hoarfrost
patuktuq	is frosted on the inside
patuqun	frosty sparkling snow
patuqutaujuq	is covered with frosty sparkling snow
paun'ngaq (*see* **ahiaq**)	blackberry (crowberry)
paun'ngaqtaqtuq	goes gathering fruit; goes berry picking
pauq	soot
pauqtuq	paddles; rows with oars

paurvik (*also* **ipulvik**)	oarlock
paut (*d.* **pautik**)	oar; paddle
pauttuq	full of soot
piannaq	playing card
piannaqatigijaa	plays cards with him/her/it
piannaqtuq	plays cards
piannauhiq	card game
piannaujaqtuk	(two) are playing cards
piaraq	young bird; young fowl
pidjarluktuq (*see*** pimmarluktuq)**	does poor work; does not do things well
piffi	dried fish
pigaaqtuq	stays up late; stays up all night
pigliqtaqtuq	bounces repeatedly
pigliqtuq	bounces once
pigliriaq	jumptrap; grasshopper
pihaaqtaa	recently got it
pihiq	drum dance song
pihudjarluktuq	limps; has difficulty walking
pihuktuq	walks
piiqtaa	takes it off; removes it
piiqtuq	it comes off; it has come off
piissak	there is none
piittuq	there is none left
pijariiqtaa	has already got it
pijumaffaaqtuq (*also*** haitaiffaaqtuq, taitaiffaaqtuq)**	wants more
pijumajaa	wants it
pijumajuq	wants; desires
pijumanngittuq	does not want...; refuses
pijumatujuq	always wants to...
pijuminaqtuq	is easy to do

pikhiktuq	bounces off
pikijuq	flies from its nest
pikiuttuq	found a nest with eggs
piksa	picture; moving picture; film; movie (from English word "picture")
piksaliun/piksaliut/piksaliuti	camera (from English word "picture")
piksaliuqtaa	takes his/her/its picture
piksasuuqtuq	goes to the movies; watches a movie (from English phrase "picture show")
piksasuurvik	movie theatre (from English phrase "picture show")
pikuk	bone between the two shoulder blades
pilagiaq (*see* ikaaraq)	an ice bridge that spans a crack in the sea ice
pilaktaa	butchers it
pilaktuq	butchers
pilaun/pilaut/pilauti (*see* havik)	butchering knife
pilgujuq	is intelligent; is bright; is smart
pilihaarniq	beginning
pilihaarnirmi	in the beginning
pilihaarnirmin/pilihaarnirmit	from the beginning
pilraaq (d. *pilraak*)	sled runner
pimattiarniq (*also* aanniaqtailiniq)	health; being healthy; staying healthy; preventing illness; taking good care of oneself
pimmariktuq	does things well; does good work; behaves well
pimmarluktuq (*see* pidjarluktuq)	is sloppy
pinahugijaa (*also* pattitigijaa)	blames him/her/it; accuses him/her/it

pingahuiqtuqtuq	does something three times
pingahuraaqtuq	catches or gets three of something
pingahut	three
pingangnalaqijuq	wind is blowing from the south
pingangnaq	south wind
Pingattiut	Wednesday
pinguatigaq	small mountain
pingujaa	pushes him/her/it
piniraq *(d. piniqqak)*	short duffle sock
pinniittuq	is ugly; is unattractive
pinniqhaqtaa	making it attractive, pretty/ beautiful
pinniqtuq	is attractive; is nice to look at
pinnirijaa	finds him/her/it attractive
piqalujaq	iceberg
piqati	partner in doing or making something
piqhilaqijuq	there is a blizzard
piqpagijaa	loves him/her/it
piqtuq	storm; blizzard
piringajuq	is bent
piritaa	bends it
pirittaaqtuq	flexible; can bend
pitikhaqtuq	shoots with an arrow
pitikhik	bow (for shooting arrows)
pitikhuqtuq	is good at shooting with a bow and arrow
pitiktaa	shoots him/her/it with an arrow
pitquhiq	habit; custom; tradition
pitquhiqtujuq	has true faith; faithful; strong faith
pitquhiqtuqtuq	always behaves like that
pitquijuq	commands, tells, orders someone to do something

pitqujaa	commands, tells, orders him/her/it to do something
pittaq	natural or human-made hole through ice
pituutaq	piece of land connecting a peninsula to the mainland; isthmus
piujaq (*also* ulapqiujaq)	toy
piujaqtuq	plays
pualrihaqtaa	shovels it
pualrihaqtuq	shovels
pualrin/pualrit/pualriti *(d. pualritiik,* pl. *pualrittit)*	shovel
pualu/pualuk	mitt
pualulik	young bearded seal with white fur; has mitts on
pualuliuqtuq	makes mitts
publak	yeast; baking soda; bubble
publakhiijuq	dough rises
publaktuq	rises; puffs up; has gas (a human)
publaumajuq	is puffed up
publiqtuq	is/has air
publiut/publiun	air pump
puhitaq	fur trim around parka hood
puhittijuq	making a sunburst (style of parka hood trim, made of wolf, from the Western Arctic)
puhittuq	boat capsized
puiguqtaa	forgets him/her/it
puiguqtuq	forgets
puijuq	surfaces to breathe
puiniq (*see* qaluiraqtuq)	fat on the top of broth
puja	dirt; grime
pujuq	smoke

pujurvik	chimney
pukaq	fine sugar snow
pukkuk	hole to pass rope through on a sled
pukkuliqhit	wood drill
pukkuq	pimple
pukukkit	pick them; pick them up
pukuktuq	picks berries; picks up small things
pulaaqtuq	visits
pulaliqtuq	it sets; it burrows
pulgiq	black person (perhaps from black Portuguese-speaking whalers)
punniq	bread
puptajuq	floats
puptan/puptat/puptati	float
putu	natural or human-made hole through something
putuguq (d. putukkuk)	big toe
putuligaq	doughnut
puudjuk	end of fingertip (mainly of thumb and index finger)
puudjuktuq	pinches
puukattaq	bag
puuvjaaqtuq (also agluqtuq)	(animal) dives under water; (animal) plunges
puvak	lung
puvalajuq	is a fat person
puvallaqtuq	gains weight
puviqqurnaqtuq/ puvitqurnaqtuq	(metal) is extremely cold
puviqhimajuq	is inflated
puviqtaq	balloon
puvittuq	swells; is swollen

puvviujaq ....

puvviujaq	bottom of amauti hood

qaajuqtuq	(living thing) is cold
qaajurnaqtuq (*see* iidji, alappaaqtuq)	cold; weather is __
qaaliruhuktuq	cold sweat and aching bones when developing a fever
qaalluviaq	main heart artery; aorta
qaamiutaq	snow platform around outside of iglu
qaammiruhuktuijuq	to patch before it wears out/opens
qaanga	the top
qaangani	on its top; above
qaangiqtaa (*see* apquhaaqtaa)	overtakes him/her/it; passes him/her/it
qaaq *(pl. qadjat)* (*see* aalliniq, alvakhaq)	caribou-skin bedding
qaatiqtuq	peels off
qablu	eyebrow
Qablunaaq	a white person
Qablunaatun/Qablunaatut	English language
Qablunaavjak	person of mixed blood, part white
qaffaktaqtuq	blinks
qaffinik ukiuqaqqa	how old is he/she/it
qaffinik ukiuqaqqit/qaffinik ukiuqaqqin	how old are you
qaffit	how many
qagaaqtuq	waves are cresting; whitecaps

qagaqtaut/qagaqtaun	firing pin of a gun; bomb
qaidjuk	give it to me; hand it over
qaijuq	comes
qainniqijuq	working on the boat; getting out of waves; beaching it; anchoring it
qajagijuq	is careful
qajainnaq	small boat
qajangnaqtuq	is dangerous because it could injure someone; fragile; requires careful handling
qajaq	boat; canoe
qajaqtuqtuq	goes by canoe; goes by kayak
qajuliuqtuq	making blood soup
qajuq	blood soup
qakipqajuq	seal is lying on the ice surface
qakkuriktuq	pure white
qakugu (*see*** qanga)**	when (in future)
qakuguliqaak	anytime (in future)
qakuguttauq	see you sometime
qakuqhijuq	turns white
qakuqtaq	white
qalahiq	belly button; navel (umbilicus)
qalairaqtuq	makes ripples
qalaktuq	has a cough; has a cold
qalaktuqtuq	coughs
qalalaqijuq	catches a cold or cough
qalingujuq (*see*** irijuq)**	has shed half its fur
qallun/qallut/qalluti	cup
qallutaujaq	toy cup/dishes
qallutaujaqtuq	playing with a tea set
qallutiqarvik	dish cupboard
qalruttaa	shoots too high
qaluiraqtuq (*see*** puiniq)**	takes the fat off the top of broth

qaluraun/qaluraut/qalurauti

qaluraun/qaluraut/qalurauti	cup; ladle
qalutaujaq	little bone below sternum/breast-bone
qalvaaq (*also* qalviaq)	young wolverine
qalviaq (*also* qalvaaq)	young wolverine
qalvik (*also* qavvik)	wolverine
qalviqut	fur trim on a parka
qamauk	toboggan
qamauktuqtuq	travels by toboggan, sled
qamittuq	is extinguished; is out (of fire or light)
qamnguinnaqtuq	habitually snores
qamnguqtuq	snores
qanait	tent frame
qanaktaq	construction framing
qanga (*see* qakugu)	when (in past)
qangiakhaq	stepnephew of a male
qangiaq	nephew of a male
qaniaq	light, soft snow
qaniaqtuq	is snowing softly
qanik	snowflake
qanikturiiktuk	(two) are adjacent; (two) are close to each other
qanilrukkut/qanilrukkun	by the shortest way
qanilrumi	nearby; close by; in the surrounding area; in the vicinity
qanilruq	surrounding area; vicinity; proximity
qaniq	mouth
qaniqtujuq	mouthy; argues a lot; is quarrelsome
qaniriktuq	is a smarty; is a smart aleck; is mouthy
qanirluktuq	has a sore mouth

qanittuq	is near
qanmaqtuq	calls the dogs
qanniq	falling snow
qanniqtuq	it snows
qanniqut	new fallen snow
qanuq	how
qanuq akituva	how much does it cost
qanuq taivakpiuk	how do you say it
qanurinnaq	any way (as in, "you can do this any way")
qanurinngittuq	is fine
qanuritpa	how is he/she/it
qanuritpit/qanuritpin	how are you (singular)
qapaktuq	has slimmed down, lost weight
qapalaqijuq	there is a whiteout
qaptirun/qaptirut/qaptiruti	fire extinguisher
qapuk	foam
qaqhauq (*see* tuullik, maliriq)	red-throated loon
qaqhuk	lower lip
qaqhuliqijuq	frowning
qaqqulaannguqtuq	has become crispy
qaqqulaaqtaa	crunches it by mouth
qaqquliuqtuq	ages fish heads under a pile of rocks
qaqquq	gamy fish head (aged under a pile of rocks)
qaqquqtuqtuq (*see* patautuqtuq)	eats gamy fish heads (aged under a pile of rocks)
qaritaq	brain
qaritaujaq	computer
qarjuq	arrow
qarjuqhaq	lure
qarliik	pants; trousers

qarmakhaliuqtuq (*also*** auviuqtuq)**	cuts snowblocks
qarmakhaq (*also*** auviq)**	snowblock
qarmakhaqtarvik (*also*** auvvivik)**	place to cut snowblocks (from the right kind of snow)
qarritijaa	brings it
qatiggaaqtuq	growls
qattaq	bucket; pail; pot
qattarjuaq (*see*** qattarjuk)**	huge pot
qattarjuk (*see*** qattarjuaq)**	barrel; drum
qattiniq	rust
qattinnaktuq	is rusted
qaujimaittuq	is numb; is dumb
qaujuq	dawns; it is daylight
qaukpat	tomorrow morning
qauq (*see*** kiinaq)**	forehead
qauqtaq	pinworm
qavvik (*also*** qalvik)**	wolverine
qiahijuq	burst into tears
qiajuq (*see*** qulviliuqtuq)**	cries
qiamiqhuqtaa	makes him/her/it cry
qian'ngaqtaq	blue fox
qian'nguqtuq	cried for so long that he/she got tired
qiblarikhijuq	is becoming shiny
qidjaktuq	has lots of gray/white hair
qidjiuqtuq	cuts wood; splits wood
qigliktaqtuq (*also*** qilgiqtaqtuq)**	jumps repeatedly
qigliktuq (*also*** qilgiqtuq)**	jumps once

qigliriaqtuq (*also* **qilgiriaqtuq**)	jumps with its hind legs (of caribou)
qihigalik	made of leather; has some leather on it
qihik	leather
qiiq	gray/white hair on a human
qijualiuqtuq	makes wood shavings
qijuk	wood
qijuktaqtuq	fetches wood
qijuvik	spruce tree
qikaaqtuq	makes a squeaking sound when walking on snow/gravel
qikiqtaq	island
qiku	clay
qilaanga	roof; ceiling
qilaaq	roof of mouth, palate; paper or snow to hide trap when trapping animals
qilak	sky; heaven
qilalugaaq	young beluga whale
qilalugaq	beluga whale
qilalugaqtuq	gets a beluga whale
qilamik	hurry up
qilamiuqtuq	hurries; hastens
qilaqqaun	snowblock that goes into top hole of an iglu
qilaudjaqtuq	does a drum dance
qilaun/qilaut/qilauti	drum
qilgiqtaqtuq (*also* **qigliktaqtuq**)	jumps repeatedly
qilgiqtuq (*also* **qigliktuq**)	jumps once
qilgiriaqtuq (*also* **qigliriaqtuq**)	jumps with its hind legs (of caribou)
qiliqtaa	ties it up (a package)
qiliqtuq	is tied up (a package)

qilirniiqtaa	unknots it; unties it
qilirniq	a knot (as in rope)
qilirniqtaa	knots it; ties it
qillukkittuq	something that you are pulling (tied up) that comes to a sudden halt
qilluq	carcass of an animal; knot in wood
qilluqiqtuq (*also* ikumajaaq)	lightning
qiluktuq	barks
qimiriaq	eyelash
qimirluk (*also* kuapikkat) (*see* qujapikkat)	backbone; spine; spinal column; vertebrae
qimirutit	drying rack for fish or meat
qimugjuk	snowdrift carved by the wind; sastrugi (from Russian "zastrugi")
qimujuittuq	dog refuses to pull
qimuktik	dogs right behind the leader
qimuktittijuq	running the dogs
qimuktuq	dog pulls
qingalik	king eider duck (male)
qingaq (*see* higguk)	nose; bird's beak; snout of a fish or animal; mosquito's proboscis
qiniqhiajaa	looks for him/her/it
qiniqhiajuq	looks for; searches
qiniqtaa	searches for him/her/it; looks for him/her/it
qinmiarjuk	young dog; puppy
qinmigiaktuq	has lots of dogs
qinmiq	dog
qinmiqpak	horse
qinmiqtuqtuq	goes by dog team
qinngaqtuq	is dazzled by the sun's reflection
qin'ngaqtuq	prays; praying

qin'ngaun/qin'ngaut/qin'ngauti	prayer
qinngarnaqtuq	dazzling
qinngijuq (*see* imannaaqtuq, niaqqulrujuq)	says no (verbally or by wrinkling nose)
qin'ngun/qin'ngut/qin'ngutik	telescope; telescopic sight; binoculars
qin'ngunmiktuq	looks through binoculars/a scope/a telescope
qin'ngurluktuq	squints; knits his/her eyebrows; frowns
qipijaa	twists it
qipik	blanket; cover
qipikhimajuq	covered with a skin, blanket, etc.
qipiktaa	covers him/her/it with a skin, blanket, etc.
qipingajuq	is twisted
qipitiqtaa/qiputiqtaa (*also* kaivjaqta)	coils it; spins it around something
Qiqaijarluarvia	May
Qiqailruq	March
qiqaujuq	is cold
qiqijuq	freezes; is frozen
qiqittiivik	freezer
qirnariktuq	black
qirnarraaqtuq	grey
qitaujaq	dress
qitiq	waist; middle
qitiqhiq	middle finger
Qitiqqautijuq	April
qitiraq	spinal cord
qitirmiut	person or people at the centre
qituhuktuq	feels like laughing
qituhungnaqtuq	is funny; is droll; is comical

qitun'ngaqtuijuq	harnessing up the dogs
qitun'ngaq	relative; relation; dog team trace line
qitun'ngaqat/qitun'ngaqatit	parents of your child's spouse
qitun'ngat	married child and their spouse
qiuvik (*also* qijuvik)	spruce tree
qiviaqtuq	looks back
qiviuq	down of bird, muskox, etc.
qivjaq	string
quagjuk	acute angle; sharp edge
quahijaaqtuq (*see* sikiiraqtuq)	skating
quana	thanks
quanaqpakpuuq	always so thankful for
quanaqpiaqqutit *(d. quanaqpiaqqutik,* pl. *quanaqpiaqquhi)*	thank you very much
quanaqqutit *(d. quanaqqutik,* pl. *quanaqquhi)*	thank you
quanaqtuq (*also* qujahuktuq)	is thankful; is grateful
quaq	frozen fish or meat
quaqhalaarun/quaqhalaarut/ quaqhalaaruti (*see* paatuliiq)	battery
quaqtaq	pinworm
qugjuk	whistling swan
quglugiaq (*see* aulvik)	small caterpillar
qugluktaaqtuq	is easy to startle
qugluktitaa	startles him/her/it
qugluktuq	is startled
quglungniq	pressure ridge
quijuq	urinates
quinaktuq	feels ticklish
quinangnaqtuq	gives a tickling sensation; makes the flesh crawl

qujagijaa	is thankful to him/her/it
qujahuktuq (*also* quanaqtuq)	is grateful; is thankful
qujajuittuq	is ungrateful
qujajuq	is content; is pleased
qujapikkak	hip bones
qukturaq *(d. ququtuqqak)*	leg; thigh
qulittaq	outside caribou-skin parka
qulliq	traditional soapstone lamp (used for cooking, heating, light); a lamp; a lantern
qulliujaq/qullikhaq	light bulb
qulvik	tear (as in crying)
qulvikhaq	iris; light bulb for flashlight
qulvijuq	tearing
qulviliuqtuq (*see* qiajuq)	cries; makes tears
qumaq	tapeworm
qumniq	crevice; small crack in ice
qunguhiniq (*also* qunguhiq)	neck
qunguhiq (*also* qunguhiniq)	neck
qunguhiqtaun	dog collar
qungujuktuq	smiles
qunmuktuq (*also* qunmuujuq)	goes up; ascends
qunmun/qunmut	upward
qunmuujuq (*also* qunmuktuq)	goes up; ascends
qun'ngiaq (*see* makpiraaq)	magazine
qun'ngiaqtuq	watches; stares at...
qupak	Delta braid; trim
qupanuaq	small bird; songbird
qupanuaqpaarjuk	horned lark
qupanuaqpak	hawk/eagle
qupilruq	worm
quppirun	barrette

quq ....

quq	urine
quriiqtaq/qurjiqtaq	yellow
qurluaqtuq	water flowing down
qurluq	waterfall
qurluqtuq	water is rushing down; Coppermine (former name of Qurluqtuq/Kugluktuk)
qurlurniq (*see* kuhirniq, hikuarniq)	icicle
qutaktuq	was unfortunate
qutangajuq	is clumsy; does not function well
qutuk	clavicle; collarbone
quuhuktuq	has to go pee
quunilaqijuq (*see* takhiqtuq, taktuktuq)	there is ice fog
quviagijaa	enjoys him/her/it
Quviahugvik	Christmas (happy time)
quviahuktuq	is happy
quviahunngittuq	is unhappy
quviahuujuq	is always happy
quvianaittuq	is unpleasant

Saaluti (*also* Havangnairvik)	Saturday
sikiiraqtuq (*see* quahijaaqtuq)	skates
sikiituuk	snowmobile
sikiituuqtuq	goes snowmobiling
sikuurvik (*also* iliharvik)	school (borrowed from English)
situa (*also* niuvirvik)	store (from English "store")

taamna	that one there
taanngaq	alcohol; alcoholic beverage; hard liquor
taaq	darkness
taaqhijuq	becomes dark
Taaqhivalirvia	July
taaqtuq	is dark
taavani	over there
tablu	chin
tablurut	cleft chin
tadja (*also* hadja)	now
tadjagu (*also* hadjagu) (*see* uvattiagu)	in a few minutes; soon; shortly
tadjaguttauq (*also* hadjaguttauq)	be right back
taffi	belt around the waist of a woman's parka
tagiuq (*also* tagjuq)	caribou noseworm; larva of throat botfly
tagiuqtuq (*also* tagjuqtuq)	sneezes
tagjaaq	ocean swell; wave
tagjuq (*also* tagiuq)	caribou noseworm; larva of throat botfly
tagjuqtuq (*also* tagiuqtuq)	sneezes
tahin'ngajuq	stretched out
tahinnuaq	small lake
tahiq	lake
tahiraq	pond; small lake
tahitaa	stretches it out

tahitirijuq	stretches something
tahittaaqtuq	can stretch
tahittuq	stretched out
tahiuqtaa	holds his/her hand
taiguaqarvik (*also* makpiraaqarvik)	library
taiguaqtaa (*also* taiguqtaa)	reads it
taiguaqtuq/taiguqtuq	reads
taiguqtaa (*also* taiguaqtaa)	reads it
taijaa	says his/her/its name
taijuq	says the name of a thing or person; names someone or something
taimaa	actually; in fact; like that
taimaaqtuq	quits; stops; gives up
taimaatun	like that
taimailiuqtuq	does so; does this; does that
taimak	stop; that's enough
taimani	at that time (in past)
taimna	that one (whose name isn't remembered; which is in a remote place or time)
taimunga (*also* nungulaittumut)	forever; without end; endless
taimuuna	at that time; a long time ago
taingna	that one over there
taitai (*also* haitai)	more; some more; again (childish language)
taitaiffaaqtuq (*also* haitaiffaaqtuq, pijumaffaaqtuq)	wants more (childish language)
tajarmiaq	bracelet
tajarniq	lower part of arm
takhijaa (*see* taktaa)	wins it; extends it
takhijuq	wins something; becomes longer

takhiqtuq (*also* taktuktuq) (*see* quunilaqijuq)	is foggy
taki	let's go; ready
takimun/takimut	lengthwise
takiunniit/takiunniin	it's okay; it doesn't matter; you're welcome
takkarjuaq	something very long
takkuani	in his presence
takkumni	in my presence
takkurni	in your presence
takkuuk	look
takpiittuq	cannot see well; is blind
takpiktuq	sees well; has good vision
taktaa (*see* takhijaa)	wins it
taktugaaluk	very foggy
taktuk	fog
taktuktuq (*also* takhiqtuq) (*see* quunilaqijuq)	is foggy
takujaa	sees him/her/it
takujuq	sees
takummarikhijaa	sees him/her/it clearly
takummarikhilimaittuq	is indistinct; is hazy; is unclear
takummarluktuq	looks wrong; looks peculiar
takunnaittuq	is invisible; is not visible
takunnaqtuq	is visible
takuttailijuq	hides; keeps from being seen
taliq (d. *tallak,* pl. *talrit*)	arm
taliqpiani	on his/her/its right side
taliqpik	right side
taliqpimni	on my right
taliqpingmuuqtuq	is right-handed
taliqpingni	on your right
taliruq	front flipper of a seal

talittuq	disappears; hides
tallimat	five
Tallimmiut	Friday
talukujaaq	curtains
taluq (*also* taluquaq)	screen or blind (for seal hunting)
taluquaq (*also* taluq)	screen (for seal hunting)
Talurjuaq/Taloyoak	resembles a big screen used for seal hunting; Spence Bay (former name)
talva	that one
talvattauq	that's all; only that
tamaffi	all of you
tamaita	all of them
tamamnuk	both of us
tamapta	all of us
tamaptik	both of you
tamatkiqtaa	took it all
tammaijaa	loses it
tammaqtuq	is lost
tamuajuq	chews continuously
tamuqtaa	chews it
tamuqtuq	chews
tamuutijaa (*see* niripkaqtaa)	chews it for him/her/it
tangmaaqtuq	camps for the night
tangmaarvik (*see* initurliq)	camp site
taqak	vein; artery; blood vessel
taqtu (d. *taqtuk*)	kidney
taqturun/taqturut/taqturuti	fat on kidneys
tariurnittuq (*also* hiipangnittuq)	salty
tarjukkuuqtuq/tariukkuuqtuq	travels by sea
tarjuliaqtuq/tariuliaqtuq	goes toward the sea
tarjuliqtuqtaa/tariuliqtuqtaa	puts salt on it

tarraq	shadow
tarraqtuqtuq	stalks an animal
tarrijaun/tarrijaut/tarrijauti	mirror
tatatirijuq	filling it up
tatatpiaqtaa	fills it up to the brim
tatattaa	fills it up
tatattuq	is full
tatijaa (*see* **pingujaa)**	pushes it back
tatilgaq	sandhill crane
tatqamna	the one inside
tatqamunga	to the inside of that one
tatqialik	cap
tatqiaq	cap brim
tatqiarikhijuq	full moon; moonlit night
tatqiq	moon
tatqiq iluittunnguqtuq	moon is full
tatqiq nappannguqtuq/tatqiq navvannguqtuq	there is a half moon
tatqiqhiun/tatqiqhiut/ tatqiqhiuti	calendar; month
Tattiarnaqtuq	October
tautuktuq	watches; looks at
tiggak	rutting male seal
tiggakhungni	smell of rutting seal
tiggutik (*also* **kingmautik)**	pliers
tigliktaa (*also* **kukiktaa)**	steals it
tigliktuq (*also* **kukiktuq)**	steals
tigluktaa	hits him/her/it with a fist
tigluun/tigluut/tigluuti	fist
tiguaq	adopted child
tiguaqhi (pl. *tiguaqhiik*)	adoptive parent
tiguaqtaa	adopts him/her/it

tiguariik	adoptive child and parent
tigumiaqtaa	carries it
tigummijaa	holds it
tigvaqtuq	goes further inland
tii	tea
tiiliuqtuq	makes tea
tiiliurun (*see* tiiliurvik)	teapot
tiiliurvik (*see* tiiliurun)	place to make tea; teapot
tiirluk	leaf tea; used tea bag
tiitaqtut (*also* kukuulaaqtuq[t])	boisterous/noisy
tiituqtuq	drinks tea
tiituquijuq	calls for tea
tikiq	index finger; thimble
tikiqqaaqhautijut (*also* uliisiqtuq)	races (borrowed from English)
tikitaa	reaches it; arrives at it
tikitqaaqhautijut	racing
tikitqaaqtuq	arrives first
tikittaqtuqtuq	approaching arrival
tikittuq	arrives
tilarrit/tilarrin/tilarriti	broom
timi	body
tingijuq	flew away (bird, insect)
tingiq	pubic hair
tingitiqtuq	starting to fly away
tingittaitkut/tingittaitkun (*also* tingittaipkut/tingittaipkun)	clothespeg; clothespin
tingittuq	flies; blows away
tingmiakkuuqtuq	goes by airplane
tingmiaq	fowl; bird
tingmiaqhiuqtuq	hunts birds
tingmiaqpak (*see* qupanuaqpak)	golden eagle

tingmiaqtuq	gets a bird by hunting
tingmijuq	is flying
tingmikhajuq	flies away; ready to take off
tingmit	plane
tinguk	liver
tipaakuun	tobacco pouch
tipaaqtuq	stinks
tipaittuq	odourless; scentless
tipi	smell; scent; odour; taste
tipigikhaut	perfume
tiriajaaq	young weasel; young ermine
tiriaq	weasel; ermine
tiriganniaq	white fox
tirikhaq	belt
tiritquq	corner; right angle
titiqqat	letters; correspondence; papers with writing on them
titiqqiqhijuq	puts up a notice
titiqqitaa	writes to him/her/it
titiqqittijuq	letter carrier; writes to someone
titiqtuut/titiqtuun	marker for making a pattern
titiraakhaq (*also* titiraakhaut/ titiraakhaun) (*see* alilajuq, titiraq)	writing paper
titiraakhaut/titiraakhaun (*also* titiraakhaq) (*see* titiraq, alilajuq)	writing paper
titirakhaq	a letter for someone
titiraq *(pl. titiqqat)*	paper; letter of the alphabet; written character
titiraqtaa	writes it
titiraqti	secretary
titiraqtuq	writes

titirarvigijaa	writes on it; writes to him/her/it
titirauhiq	handwriting/writing system
titiraujaqtuq	draws
titiraun/titiraut/titrauti	pen; pencil
titqalaaqtuq	sailing; blowing away
titqalaarut/titqalaut/titqautaq	sail
titqaun/titqaut/titqauti (*also* **kivvin/kivvit/kivviti**)	weight for a fishnet
titqiaq	the brim of a cap
tiuqtiuqtuq	a bird chirps; a bird twitters
tivjaq	driftwood; anything that drifted ashore
tivjaqtaqtuq (*see* qijuktaqtuq)	fetches driftwood
tivjariktuq	tasty; good tasting; has a nice scent
tivjarluktuq	bad taste/smell (of pipe tobacco)
tivjat	driftwood
tuattuq	narrow
tuffijuq	finds tracks
tuffiuqtuq/tumihiuqtuq	looks for tracks
tugliq	the second one; the next one
tugliqti	second lead dog
tugliqtik	dogs right behind the qimuktik
tuhaajaa	hears him/her/it (continuous sound); understands him/her/it
tuhaajuq	hears (a continuous sound); understands
tuhaqtaa	hears him/her/it (short sound)
tuhaqtuq	hears (a short sound)
tuharnaarnaqtuq	is nice to listen to
tuhugijaa	is envious of him/her/it
tuhujuq	is envious
tuhunnaq	lucky; I'm envious

tuhutujuq	is always envious
tui *(d. **tuik**)*	shoulder
tukhiqtuq	asks for something; begs for something
tukhuktaa	dents it
tukhungajuq	is dented
tukkaliqtuq	kicking a dying animal; person kicking; the thumps of a rabbit's foot
tukkaqtaa	kicks it with his/her foot
tukkaqtuq	kicking
tuktu	caribou
tuktuttuq	gets a caribou
tuktuujaq	daddy-long-legs spider
tuktuvak	moose
tuktuvalik *(d. **tuktuvallak**)*	moosehide sole
tulagvik (*see* **apurvik, niudjivik**)	dock
tulaktuq (*see* **apuqtuq**)	boat reaches the shore; boat lands
tulimaaq	rib
tulrujuq	has long, shaggy hair; has thick hair
tulugaq	raven
tuluriaq	canine tooth
tumi	track; footprint
tungauttuq	shoots too low
tungmiqqat (*also* **aluijarvik**) (*see* **aalliraq**)	stairs
tungujuktuq	purple
tungullaktuq	is exhausted
tunguttuq	turns blue (a person, from being cold, choking...)
tunihijuq	gives something
tunijaa	gives it

tunin'nguiqtirijuq ....

tunin'nguiqtirijuq	kills time
tunin'nguitkutikhaq	pastime; hobby
tunmiraq (*see* majuraun, majurautaq)	step ladder; piece of skin laid on the ice when seal hunting
tunmirarijaa	uses it to climb up
tunmirautit	stairs
tunnuq	caribou fat
tunnuriktuq	lots of caribou fat; fat caribou
tunu	back
tunuani	behind him/her/it
tunuhiniq	nape of the neck
tunuhitaq	first stomach of caribou; rumen
tunujaq	eyelid
tunulliq	the one farthest behind
tunutaa	turns his/her/its back to him/her/it
tunuttuq	turns his/her/its back
tupaaqtaa	wakes him/her/it up
tupagiaqtuq	wakes up early
tupagumitaaqtuqtuq	has breakfast
tupakhaqtaa	wakes him/her/it up (in a rough manner)
tupaktuq	wakes up (early); gets up from sleeping
tupikhaq	tent canvas
tupilak	devil
tupiq	tent
tupiqtuq	has set up a tent
tupiqtuqtuq	sets up a tent
tupittuq	chokes
tupqijuq	making a tent
tuqhualiqiji	plumber
tuqhuaq (*also* paipak)	pipe

tuqhuuk	porch
tuqujuq	dies
tuqulrajaqtuq (*also*** tuqutqajaktuq)**	almost dies
tuqungajuq	is dead
tuqutaa	kills him/her/it
tuqutaujuq	was killed
tuqutqajaktuq (*also*** tuqulrajaqtuq)**	almost dies
tuquttijuq (*see*** inuaqtuq)**	kills someone/something
tuudjaarnaqtuq	hurts the foot through sole of soft boots
tuugaaq	tusk
tuulligiaq	golden plover
tuullik (*see*** qaqhauq, maliriq)**	yellow-billed loon; king loon
tuuq	ice chisel
tuuqtaa	chisels it
tuuqtuq	works with a chisel
tuurmiaq	stranger; foreigner
tuutaujaq	button
tuvaaq (pl. *tuvirrat***)**	hunter on ice
tuvak	landfast ice floe
tuvjaqhijuq	follows tracks
tuvjaqtuq	tracks an animal; follows an animal's trail

Ualinirmiut	Western Arctic Inuit

uanmun	westward
uaqhijuq	washes something
uaqhin/uaqhit/uaqhiti	washing machine
uaqhivik	sink
uaqtaa	washes him/her/it
uaqtakhat	dirty laundry
uaqtiqtuq (*also* uaqtuq)	washes himself/herself/itself; bathes
uaqtuq (*also* uaqtiqtuq)	washes himself/herself/itself; bathes
uataa	west side
uataani	in the west
ublaaq (*see* ublaigami)	morning; this morning
ublaigami (*see* ublaaq)	this morning
ublaigumi	this afternoon; later on today/tonight
ublu	nest
Ubluiqtirvia	December
ubluliuqtuq	makes a nest
ublumi	today
ublumittauq	see you later today
ubluq	day
ubluqhiun/ubluqhiut/ ubluqhiuti	wristwatch; clock
ubluqqukhijuq	short day
Ubluqtuhinia	January
ubluqtujuq	long day
ubluriaq	star
ugjugalik/ugjugallak	boot with a sole made from bearded seal
ugjugaq/ugjuaq	young bearded seal
ugjuk	bearded seal
uhiijaqtuq	unloads

uhiijaut	barge
uhiliqpallaaqtuq	is overloaded
uhin'ngajuq (*see*** uhiqtuq)**	is naked; is undressed; has no clothes on
uhiqtiqtuq (*also*** aannuraangijaqtuq)**	takes off his/her own clothes; undresses
uhiqtuq (*see*** aannuraangiqtuq)**	is undressed; is naked
uhuilitaq	protective sheath, made of fur, for male dog's penis (to prevent freezing)
uhuk	penis
ui/uik	husband
uilgahuk	spinster; unmarried woman
uilgaqtuq	she is a widow
uilgarniq	widow
uilik	married woman
uingaiqtaa (*also*** kangiqhijaa)**	understands him/her/it
uingaiqtuq	understands
uingairnaqtuq (*see*** kangiqhihurnaqtuq)**	is easy to understand; is understandable
uingajuq	is naive; cannot understand
uiniq	open lead in ice created by winter wind
uipkuaq	fishing line
uirniq	curved tip of sled runner
uitajuq/uittuq	has his/her/its eyes open
uitapqaqtuq	half opens his/her/its eyes
ujarak	stone; rock
ujaraktujuq	rocky area
ujaraliaq	stones; gravel
ujuruk	niece of a male
ujurukhaq	stepniece of a male
ukalaaq	young hare

ukaliq	hare
ukharjuk/aputtaaq	snowbank
ukhuviaqtaq	boot made from caribou skin with fur on the inside
ukiakhaq	early fall
ukiaq	fall; autumn
ukiijuq	spends the winter
ukiuq	year; winter
ukiuqtuq	winter has arrived
ukkuaq	door
ukkuaqtuq	closes the door
ukkuiqtuq	opens the door
ukpatik	buttocks of an animal
ukpik	snowy owl
ukpirijaa	believes him/her/it
ukpirnaqtuq	it is believable; trustworthy
ukua	this one
ukuak	these two
ukuaq (*compare* angajun'nguq, nukaun'nguq)	daughter-in-law of a female; sister-in-law of a female
ukuariik	daughter-in-law and mother-in-law together
ukuat	these three (or more)
ukujuq	bows; bends forward
ukutitaq	jackknife
ulapqijuq	plays
ulapqiujaq (*also* piujaq)	toy
ulapqiujaqtuq	plays with a toy
uligaaq (*also* ulik)	blanket
uliisiqtuq (*also* tikiqqaaqhautijut)	races (borrowed from English)
ulik (*also* uligaaq)	blanket

uliktaa	covers him/her/it with a blanket; puts a blanket on him/her/it
uliktuq	covers himself/herself/itself with a blanket
ulimakkak	rat
ulin'ngajuq	inside out
ulipkaaqtaa	tide
ulipkaaqtuq	is filled up to overflowing
uliuhiniq	fillet (of meat)
uliut/uliun	sinew, before it becomes ivalu
ulruaqhijuq	staggers
ulrujuq	falls; topples over
ulu	woman's knife
uluadjaktuq	has frozen cheeks
uluagullik	Canada goose
uluak/uludjak/uludjat	cheek
uluaqtaa	saws it
uluaqtuqtaa	saws it up
uluaqtuun	saw
uluaraqtuq (*also* agiraqtuq)	plays a fiddle, violin
uluaraut (*also* agiraq)	fiddle, violin
ulukhaqtuuq	has lots of soapstone (also the traditional name for Holman Island)
uluriahuktuq	feels a pain
ulurianaqtuq	is painful
umialik	one who has a boat
umiaq	boat
umiaqpak	ship
umik	beard
umiktuq	is closed
umilik	has a beard
umilruk	both lips

umingmaaq	young muskox
umingmak	muskox
Umiujaq	Peterhead
umngijaqtuq	shaves
umngijauti	razor
una	this one here
unaaq	harpoon shaft
unaguiqhiqtuq	rests
Unaguiqhirvik (*also*** Hanahuilrun/Hanahuilrut)**	Sunday
unaguittuq	is not tired; tireless
unaguqtaiqhajait	trains dogs by adding them to a dog team; partly trained dogs
unaguqtuq	is tired; is sleepy
ungahiaqtuq	is further away
ungahikhijuq	gets further away
ungahikkutigiiktut	are equally far apart
ungahiktuq	is far away
ungahitqijaq (*also*** avalliq)**	the one farthest away
ungalaq	west wind
ungalaqtuq	wind is blowing from the west
ungalliq	the farthest one; the most distant one
ungataani	beyond him/her/it
ungirlaaq	bag made from whole animal skin to store food
ungirun/ungirut/ungiruti	drawstring around top of boot
ungullaun/ungullaut/ ungullauti	dog whip
uniaqtaa	drags him/her/it; pulls him/her/it
uniaqti	last dog in the team
uniaqtik	dogs right next to the sled
uniaqtuq	drags

uningajuq	is voracious; is greedy
unipkaaq	story; legend
unipkaaqtuq	tells a legend; tells a story
uniq	armpit
un'nguq	wart
unnirluktuq	tattles; gossips
unnuaq	night; last night
unnuffaaqqat	tomorrow evening
unnuk	evening
unnukpan/unnukpat	tonight; when night falls
unnuktuq	night has fallen
unnuliqtuq	night is falling
unuqtuq	a child fights, makes faces, etc.
upaktaa	rejoins him/her/it; catches up to him/her/it; goes to see him/her/it
upalungaijaqtuq (*also* **hannaijaqtuq; itqanaijaqtuq; parnaijaqtuq**)	gets ready
upin'ngaaq	spring
upin'ngakhaq	early spring
upin'ngaqhiqtuq	is caught off guard; is surprised
upin'ngaqtaa	he surprised him/her/it
uqaallautijaa	tells him/her/it
uqajuittuq	is mute; cannot speak
uqamaluktuq	mumbles; grumbles
uqaq	tongue
uqaqatigijaa	talks with him/her/it
uqaqti	spokesperson
uqaqtuq	speaks; talks
uqarvigijaa	talks to him/her/it
uqauhiq	word; language; speech
uqauhirijaa	talks about him/her/it
uqaujaq (*see* **atungaujaq**)	leaf

uqautijaa	speaks to him/her/it
uqhuq	blubber; whale fat; oil
uqhuqarvik	fuel tank
uqhurjualiqiji	fuel delivery person
uqhurjuaq	fuel oil
uqhurjuaqtaun/uqhurjuaptaut/ uqhurjuaqtauti/uqhurjuaqtaut	fuel truck
uqittuq	is light (weight)
uqpik (*see* avaalaqiaq)	willow
uqpiliurniq (*see* avaalaqiaq)	making a sleeping mat out of willows
uqqarikhijuq	speaks better; has improved his/her speech
uqqariktuq	speaks well
uqquani	on the leeward side
uqquaq	a place that is out of the wind; the leeward side of a hill
uqquujuq	keeps warm
uqquuqun/uqquuqut/ uqquuquti (*see* uunaqun)	heater; something that provides warmth
uquiqtuq/uqquiqtuq	is no longer warm
uquittuq/uqquittuq	is not warm; does not stay warm
uqumaittuq	is heavy
uqummiaq (*also* nungulaaq)	candy
uqummiaqtaa	keeps it in his/her/its mouth
uqumuujuq	travels with the wind; fair wind
uquutaq	windbreak
uriaqtuq/uriuqtuq	spits out
urjuk	moss
urviujaq (*also* imiraqtuun)	bowl
utajuraq	small seal
utaqqijaa/nutaqqijaa	waits for him/her/it
utaqqijuq (*also* nutaqqijuq)	waits

utaqqiuqtaa (*also* **nutaqqiuqtaa**)	waits for him/her/it
utimuktuqtuq	goes backwards
utimun/utimut (*see* **kingumun/ kingumut**)	on the way back; backwards
utimuujuq/utimuuqtuq	heading homeward
utiqtuq	returns
utkuhik	cooking pot (traditionally made of soapstone)
utkuhikhaq/ukkuhikhaq	soapstone (for making cooking pots)
uttuk	vagina
utuqqaq	something old
uugaq	tomcod
uujuq	boiled meat
uuktaun/uuktaut/uuktauti (*see* **uuktuun**)	ruler
uuktuqtaa	measures him/her/it; tries it on; samples it
uuktuqtuq	measures; tries something; samples something
uuktuun/uuktuut/uuktuuti (*see* **uuktaun**)	ruler; pattern; example; sample
uulijuq	shivers; shakes
uumman/uummat/uummati	heart
uunaqtuq (*see* **aumaallaktuq**)	is hot
uunaqun (*see* **uqquuqun**)	furnace
uunnaalaqijuq	warms up
uunnaaqtuq	is lukewarm
uutiqtittuq	burns himself/herself/itself
uvaguk	we; the two of us
uvagut	we; the three or more of us
uvamnik	me
uvamnit	from me

uvanga ....

uvanga	I
uvattiagu (*see* tadjagu, hadjagu)	later
uvattiaguttauq	see you later
uvattiannuaq	a little while ago
uvattiaq	a few minutes ago
uviluq	seashell
uvinik	epidermis; human skin
uvva	here it is; here she is; here he is

English
to
Inuinnaqtun

A

abandoned child	iliarjuk
absent-minded	ihumaittuq
accompanies him/her	inuuqatigijaa
accountant	maniliqiji
accuses him/her/it	pinahugijaa; -niraq-; (*old word*: pattitigijaa)
across; *goes* ___	ikaaqtuq; itivjaaqtuq
across; *goes* ___ *it*	ikaaqtaa
action or words; *person whose* ___ *are the same as his/her namesake*	atiqtujuq
actually	taimaa
added on (also jumpsuit)	atajuq
adjacent; *they (two) are* ___	qanikturiiktuk
adopted child	tiguaq
adoptive child and parent	tiguariik
adoptive parent	tiguaqhi (pl. *tiguaqhiik*)
adoptive parents	tiguaqhiik
adopts him/her/it	tiguaqtaa
adult	inirniq
adult; *young* ___	inirnikhaq
adultery; *commits* ___	aallatuqtuq
afraid; *is* ___	iqhijuq; kappiahuktuq
afraid; *is* ___ *of him/her/it*	kappiagijaa; iqhigijaa
afraid; *is* ___ *to go on ice, boat, or plane*	nangiaqtuq
afraid; *is not* ___ *to go on ice, boat, or plane*	nangiaqtuittuq/nangiaqtujuittuq
afterbirth	alraaq
afternoon; *this* ___	ublaigumi
again; *see you* ___ *sometime*	ilaanittauq; ilaanilu; qakuguttauq

against; *are ___ each other*	hanmitijuk
against; *is ___ someone/something*	hanmijuq
age; *person of the same ___*	inuuqati; aippaq
aged seal/walrus fat	igunaq
aged seal/walrus meat in fat	igunaq
ages fish heads under rocks	qaqquliuqtuq
ago	
ago; *a few minutes ___*	uvattiaq
ago; *a little while ___*	uvattiannuaq
ago; *a long time ___*	ingilraan
ago; *some time ___*	imani
agreement; *is in ___*	angiqhimajuq
agrees	angiqtuq
ahead; *go ___*	akhun
ahead; *is ___ of him/her/it*	hivulirijaa
aims at something with a gun (or other object)	kijuaqtuqtuq
air; *is/has ___*	publiqtuq
airplane; *goes by ___*	tingmiakkuuqtuq
airport	mittarvik
airstrip	milvik/mivvik
alarmed; *is ___*	kappiahuktuq; iqhijuq
alarming; *is ___*	kappianaqtuq
alcohol	taanngaq
alcohol; *wood/medicinal ___ (not for drinking)*	ikkikhan/ikkikhat/ikkikhati/ ikkikhaun(t)
alive; *is ___*	inuujuq
all of them	tamaita
all of us	tamapta
all of you	tamaffi
all; *that's ___*	talvattauq
all; *took it ___*	tamatkiqtaa
alone; *is ___*	avaliittuq
alone; *stays ___*	kihimngiuqtuq

alone; *wants to be* ___	kihimngiurumajuq
already; *has* ___ *got it*	pijariiqtaa
alright; *is* ___	naammaktuq
amauti; *bottom of* ___ *hood*	puvviujaq
amazing; *is* ___	arlingnaqtuq
amulet	attatak
anchor	kihaq
anchored; *is* ___	kihaqtuq
anchored; *is well* ___	kihadjariktuq
anchoring it	qainniqijuq
angle; *acute* ___	quagjuk
angle; *right* ___	tiritquq
angry; *is* ___	ningahuktuq
angry; *never gets* ___	mamiahujuittuq
animal flying or running away	niviuqtujuq
animal; *domestic* ___	pamiqhaaq
animal; *game* ___	anngun
animal; *male* ___	anguhalluq
animal; *tame, unafraid* ___	nujuittuq
animal; *untamed* ___	nujuaqtujuq
ankle	hingirniq
annoyed; *is* ___	mamiahuktuq
annoying; *is* ___	palvinaqtuq
another one	aalla
another; *in* ___ *place*	ahiani
answers	kiujuq
answers him/her/it	kiujaa
antler	nagjuk
antlers; *gores it with* ___ *or horns*	nagjungmiktaa
anus	itiq
anvil	kaugvik
any way (as in, "you can do this any way")	qanutuinnaq

anytime (in future)	qakuguliqaak
anywhere	humiliqaak
apart; *are equally far* ___	ungahikkutigiiktut
apart; *comes* ___	ataiqtuq
apart; *is taken* ___	angivittuq/itumittuq
appear; *begins to* ___	hatqummiqhijuq
appears	hatqummiqtuq
April	Qitiqqautijuq
apron	haamirun
argues a lot	qaniqtujuq
arm	taliq (d. *tallak,* pl. *talrit*)
arm; *lower part of* ___	tajarniq
arm; *upper* ___	akhatquq
armpit	uniq
around	avataani
around; *goes* ___ *something*	kaivaluaqtuq
arrival; *approaching* ___	tikittaqtuqtuq
arrives	tikittuq
arrives at it	tikitaa
arrives before him/her/it	hivulirijaa
arrives first	tikitqaaqtuq
arrow	qarjuq
arrow; *shoots him/her/it with an* ___	pitiktaa
arrow; *shoots with an* ___	pitikhaqtuq
arrowhead	natquq
artery	taqak
ash	arja
ashbin	arjaijarvik (*see* arjakuurvik)
ashtray	arjakuurvik; higaakuvik (*see* arjaijarvik)
aside; *puts it* ___ *for someone*	minittailijaa
asking; *he was* ___ *for it*	manittuq
asks	apiqhuqtuq

asks a question	apiqhijuq
asks for information	apiqhuijuq
asks for something	tukhiqtuq
asks him/her/it	apirijaa
asleep; *falls* ___	hinaaqhijuq
attacks	hurjuktuq
attractive; *finds him/her/it* ___	pinnirijaa
attractive; *is* ___	pinniqtuq
attractive; *making it* ___	pinniqhaqtaa
August	Niqiliqivik
aunt (father's sister, not mother's sister)	attak (*see* arnarvik)
aunt (mother's sister, not father's sister)	arnarvik (*see* attak)
autumn	ukiaq
axe	atuaqtaun/atuaqtaut/atuaqtauti

baby bottle	amaamaun/amaamaut/amaamauti; maamaun/maamaut/maamauti
baby bottle; *cap under lid of* ___ *to prevent leaking*	muluilitaq
baby; *newborn* ___	mirraaq
bachelor	nuliilgahuk
back	tunu
back; *on the way* ___	utimun/utimut
back; *turns his/her/its* ___	tunuttuq
back; *turns his/her/its* ___ *to him/her/it*	tunutaa
backbone	qimirluk; kuapikkat (sg. *kuapigaq*)

backpack	nangmaktaq
backwards	utimun/utimut; kingumun/kingumut
backwards; *goes* ___	utimuktuqtuq
bad dream	hinnarluktuq
bad; *does a* ___ *job*	pidjarluktuq; pimmarluktuq
bad; *is* ___	nakuunngittuq
bag	puukattaq
bag made from whole animal skin to store food	ungirlaaq
bait on a hook	mikkirun
baking soda	publak
bald; *has gone* ___	nujaiqtuq
baleen	huqqaq
ball	muqpak
balloon	puviqtaq
bannock	muqpaujaq
barge	uhiijaut
bark at each other aggressively	halraqtuk
bark of tree	amiraq
barks	qiluktuq; halraqtuq
barometer	hilahiun/hilahiut/hilahiuti
barrette	quppirun
bathes	uaqtiqtuq; uaqtuq
bathing suit	naluujauti
bathroom	anarvik
battery	paatuliiq; quaqhalaarun/ quaqhalaarut/quaqhalaaruti
bay	kangiqhuk
be right back	hadjaguttauq/tadjaguttauq
beaching it	qainniqijuq
beak	higguk
beak; *long-* ___ *ed or long-nosed animal*	higguqquqtujuq
bear; *gets a polar* ___	nanuqtuq

bear; *polar* ___	nanuq
bear; *polar* ___ *den*	apittiuvik; apittaaq
bear; *young polar* ___	nanuaq
bearberry	kablaq
bearberry/crowberry leaves (for tea)	kablaqutit
beard	umik
beard; *has a* ___	umilik
beautiful	pinniqhaqtaa
beaver	kigiaq
becomes different	aallannguqtuq
bed	igliq
bed; *goes to* ___	innaqtuq
bedding; *caribou-skin* ___	qaaq (pl. *qadjat*) (*see* aalliniq, alvakhaq, alvat)
bedroom	hinigvik
bee	iguttaq
before him/her/it	hivuani
before; *that which has gone* ___	hivuniq
beginning; *from the* ___	pilihaarnirmin/pilihaarnirmit
beginning; *in the* ___	pilihaarnirmi
beginning; *the* ___	pilihaarniq
begs for something	tukhiqtuq
behaves well	pimmariktuq
behaves; *always* ___ *like that*	pitquhiqtuqtuq
behind him/her/it	tunuani
behind; *the one farthest* ___	tunulliq
believable; *it is* ___	ukpirnaqtuq
believes him/her/it	ukpirijaa
bell	hivajaun/hivajaut/hivajauti
belly	nadjak (*see* aqiaruq)
belly button	qalahiq
belly; *lower part of* ___	aqiamuk
belly; *skin and flesh of* ___	aqiaviniq

belt	tirikhaq
belt around the waist of a woman's parka	taffi
bend; *can* ___	pirittaaqtuq
bends forward	ukujuq
bends it	piritaa
bent; *is* ___	piringajuq
berries; *picks* ___	ahiaqtaqtuq; paun'ngaqtaqtuq
berries; *prepares* ___	ahidjijuq
berry	ahiaq
berry; *black* ___ *(also crow)*	paun'ngaq
berry; *bear* ___	kablaq
beside him/her/it	haniani
between; *goes in* ___	akulrutaaqtuq
between; *is located in* ___	akunnganiittuq
between; *space in* ___	akunniq
beyond him/her/it	avataani; ungataani
bias tape (solid colour)	ikhikhaq
bicep	kattuaq
big	angijuq; -qpak; -rjuaq
biggest; *the* ___ *one*	angitqijaq
bile	hunagaq
binoculars	qin'ngun/qin'ngut/qin'ngutik
binoculars; *looks through* ___	qinngunmiktuq
birch; *dwarf* ___	uqpik (*see* avaalaqiaq)
bird	tingmiaq
bird; *gets a* ___ *by hunting*	tingmiaqtuq
bird; *small* ___	qupanuaq
bird; *young* ___	piaraq
birds; *hunts* ___	tingmiaqhiuqtuq
birth; *gives* ___ *to a child*	nutaqqijuq; utaqqijuq
birthday	annivik
birthday; *is his/her/its* ___	annivilittuq

biscuit	hiqulaaq
bitch (female dog)	arnaaqutaq/arnalluq
bites him/her/it	kiijaa
bites someone/something	kiihijuq
black	qirnariktuq
blackberry (crowberry)	paun'ngaq
black person	pulgiq (probably from the word Portuguese due to Portuguese-speaking black whalers)
blackfly	milugiaq
bladder	nakahuk
blade; *shoulder* ___	kiahik (d. kiattik)
blades; *bone between the two shoulder* ___	pikuk
blames him/her/it	pinahugijaa; -niraq-; (*old word*: pattitigijaa)
blanket	uligaaq; ulik; qipik
blanket; *covers himself/herself/itself with a* ___	uliktuq
blanket; *puts a* ___ *on him/her/it*	uliktaa
bleeding; *stops* ___	auguiqtuq; aunaaruiqtuq
bleeds (monthly)	aunaaqtuq
bleeds from the nose	auglaqijuq
blind; *is* ___	takpiittuq
blinks	qaffaktaqtuq
blizzard	piqtuq
blizzard; *there is a* ___	piqhilaqijuq
blood	auk
blood clot	augiaq
blood soup	qajuq
blood vessel	taqak
blood; *is covered with* ___	aunginnannguqtuq
blood; *spits* ___	adjiqijuq
blood soup; *making* ___	qajuliuqtuq

blowing away	titqalaaqtuq
blows away	tingittuq
blubber	uqhuq
blubber; *aged* ___ (used to dip food in)	mihuraq/mihuraaq
blue	arjiqtaq
blue; *turns* ___ (a person, from being cold, choking...)	tunguttuq
blueberry	kigutigingnaq/kigutangirnaq
blushed; turned red	aupadjaktuq
board; *gets on* ___	ikijuq
board; *helps him/her/it on* ___	ikipkaqtaa
board; *is on* ___	ikimajuq
board; *puts him/her/it on* ___	ikijaa
boat	umiaq
boat capsized	puhittuq
boat; *one who has a* ___	umialik
boat; *small* ___	qajainnaq
boat; *working on the* ___	qainniqijuq
body	timi
body; *limbs of the* ___	avatait
boil; *a* ___	ajuaq
boisterous	kukuulaaqtuq(t); tiitaqtut
bold; *is* ___	alguangajuq
bomb	qagaqtaut/qagaqtaun
bone	hauniq
bone for gnawing or picking	kipkaq
bone with meat and fat, good for gnawing or picking	kipkariktuq
bone; *gnaws on it* (a bone)	kipkaqtaa
bone; *hip* ___	hilviaq
bone; *little* ___ *below sternum/ breastbone*	qalutaujaq
book	makpiraaq

boot	kamik (d. kammak, pl. kamngit)
boot made from caribou skin with fur on inside	ukhuviaqtaq
boot with a sole made from bearded seal	ugjugalik/ugjugallak
boot; *fancy* ___	hivuralik (d. hivurallak)
boots; *has his/her* ___ *or shoes on*	kamiktuq
boots; *puts his/her* ___ *or shoes on*	kamiktuqtuq
boots; *takes his/her* ___ *or shoes off*	kamiijaqtuq
boots; *waterproof* ___	ipirautik
border	kigliq
border; *on its* ___	kiglingani
bored; *is* ___ *by him/her/it*	alianaigijaa
born; *is* ___	anijuq
both of us	tamamnuk
both of you	tamaptik
bothersome; *is* ___	palvinaqtuq
bottle	hikuliaq
bottle; *baby* ___	amaamaun/amaamaut/amaamauti; maamaun/maamaut/maamauti
bounces off	pikhiktuq
bounces once	pigliqtuq
bounces repeatedly	pigliqtaqtuq
boundary	kigliq
bow (for shooting arrows)	pitikhik
bowhead whale	arviq (*see* arvaaq)
bowhead; *young* ___ *whale*	arvaaq (*see* arviq)
bowl	imiraqtuun; urviujaq
bowlegged	iblungajuq/iplungajuq
bows	ukujuq
box; *grub* ___	hiurjuun/hiurjuut/hiurjuuti
boy	angun/angut/anguti
boy; *teenaged* ___	inuuhuktuq
boy/girlfriend; *your* ___	hanngiutit

bracelet	tajarmiaq
brain	qaritaq
branch of a tree	ihaqutaq (pl. ihaqutait)
brant; *black* ___	nirlirnaq
brass	havilhaq; havikhaq
brassiere	iviangiilitaq
brave	nangiaqtuittuq/nangiaqtujuittuq
bread	punniq; muqpaujaq
breakfast; *has* ___	tupagumitaaqtuqtuq
breaks	naviktuq
breaks it	naviktaa
breaks; *a wave* ___ *against the shore*	hiqqaqtuq
breast	iviangiq *(d. iviangik)*
breastbone	hakiaq
breath	anirniq
breath; *is out of* ___	anngajuktuqtuq; anrajuktuq
breathe; *surfaces to* ___	puijuq
breathes	aniqhaaktuq
breathing hole; *a seal's* ___	aglu
breezy; *is* ___	anughaaqtuq
brim of a cap	titqiaq
brings him/her/it	agjaqtaa
brings it	qarritijaa
brings it somewhere else	haniqpaijuq
brings something	agjaqtuq
broken; *a piece of a* ___ *object*	navvaq
broken; *is* ___	navikhimajuq; ahiruqtuq
broom	haqiktaun/haqiktaut/haqiktauti; tilarrin/tilarrit/tilarriti
broth	imiraq
broth; *fat on top of* ___	puiniq *(see qaluiraqtuq)*
brother of a female	ani/anik

brother; *older* ___ *of a male;* (older sibling, same sex)	angajuk
brother; *older step* ___ *of a male*	angajukhaq
brother; *younger* ___ *of a female*	aqqaluaq (*compare* ani)
brother; *younger* ___ *of a male*	nukaq
brother; *younger step* ___ *of a male*	nukakhaq
brother; *younger step* ___ *of a female*	aqqaluakhaq (*compare* anikhaq)
brother-in-law (husband of wife's younger sister)	ningauk
brother-in-law of a male (husband of wife's younger sister)	nukaun'nguq (compare angajun'nguq)
brother-in-law of a male (husband of wife's older sister)	angajun'nguq (*see* nukaun'nguq, ukuaq)
brown	kajuqtuq; marlungajuq
brushes his/her/its teeth	kigutigikhaqtuq; kiguhiqijuq
bubble	publak
bucket	qattaq
bug repellent	kikturiijaun/kikturiijaut/kikturiijauti
builder; *house* ___	igluliuqti
bull of caribou, muskox, etc.	pangniq
bullet shell	kinguniq
bullet tip/arrowhead	natquq
buries him/her/it (a body)	iluviqtaa
buries it	haujaa
burn; *starts* ___*ing*	ikuallaktuq
burning; *is* ___	ikumajuq; ikualaaqtuq
burns down/up	ikualajuq
burns himself/herself/itself	uutiqtittuq
burns wood	aumaliuqtuq
burnt; *is* ___	algiqtuq
burnt; *smells* ___	algirnilaqijuq
burps	nikhaaktuq
burrow	hiti

burrow; *digs a* ___	hitiliuktuq
burst out laughing	iglahiktuq
busy; *is* ___	hanaqijuq
busy; *keeps* ___	aliiquhiqtuq
butchering wildlife	niqiliqijuq
butchers	pilaktuq
butchers it	pilaktaa
butter	paja/pata
butterfly	haqalikitaaq
butter knife	pataliqhit/pataliqhin; pajaliqin
buttock; *human* ___	iqquk; nuluq (d. *nulluk*)
buttock; *side of* ___	mimiq
buttocks; *animal* ___	ukpatik
button	tuutaujaq
buys	niuviqtuq
buys it	niuviqtaa
by; is ___ *himself*	kihimmiuqtuq
by the outside	hilataagut

calendar	tatqiqhiun/tatqiqhiut/tatqiqhiuti
calf of a caribou, muskox, etc.	nurraq
calf of a leg	nakahungnaq
calls for tea	tiituquijuq
camera	piksaliun/piksaliut/piksaliuti
camp site	tangmaarvik (*see* initurliq)
camp site (old)	initurliq (*see* tangmaarvik)

camping area; *old* ___ (where a tent has been pitched)	nunaturliq
camps for the night	tangmaaqtuq
can opener	angmaqtirun
candle	ikummat; patqujaq
candle ice	illaujaq
candy	uqummiaq; nungulaaq
cannot	ajuqtuq
canoe	qajaq
canoe; *goes by* ___	qajaqtuqtuq
cap	tatqialik
cap; *baby bottle* ___ *under lid, to prevent leaking (also nipple protector, fur)*	muluilitaq
cap brim	tatqiaq
capelin	angmagiaq
captain of a boat	aquti
car	akhaluun/akhaluut/akhaluuti
car; *goes by* ___ *or truck*	akhaluutikkuuqtuq
carcass; *animal* ___	qilluq
card (from a deck of cards)	piannaq
card game	piannauhiq
cards; *plays* ___	piannaqtuq
cards; *plays* ___ *with him/her/it*	piannaqatigijaa
cards; *(two) are playing* ___	piannaujaqtuk
care; *someone you really* ___ *about*	iviurnauti
care; *takes good* ___ *of*	pamiqhihuktuq
careful; *is* ___	qajagijuq
careful; *requires* ___ *handling*	qajangnaqtuq
caribou	tuktu
caribou calf	nurraq
caribou fat	tunnuq
caribou; *bull* ___	pangniq
caribou; *fat* ___	tunnuriktuq

caribou; *female* ___ (cow)	kulavak
caribou; *gets a* ___	tuktuttuq
caribou; *young female* ___	nurraittuarjuk
caribou; *young male* ___	nukatugaq
caribou calf; *year old* ___	nukatukkaaq
caribou fat; *lots of* ___	tunnuriktuq
caribou-skin blanket	alvat; qaaq (*see* aalliniq)
carpenter; *a* ___	hanaji
carries a baby on his/her back	amaaqtuq
carries him/her/it	agjaqtaa
carries it	tigumiaqtaa
carries something	agjaqtuq
carries something on his/her/its shoulders	kakaktuq
carries something on the back	nangmaktuq
carry; *they (two)* ___ *something together*	akiraqatigiiktuk
casket	iluvirvik
cassette tape	atuqtuujaq; nipikhaun
catches a game animal	angujuq
catches it (*a game animal*)	angujaa
catches up to him/her/it	upaktaa
caterpillar; *small hairy* ___	quglugiaq; aulvik
caught off guard; *is* ___	upinngaqhiqtuq
CD	atuqtuujaq
ceiling	qilaanga
centre; *people from the* ___	qitirmiut (*old spelling*: kitikmeot)
chain or rope to tie dogs or boats	ipiutaq
chair	ikhivautaq
challenges someone to a game	akihaqtuq
changed; *has* ___	aallangajuq
changes	aallannguqtuq
char; *Arctic* ___	iqalukpik
char; *big* ___	hinmiutaq

char; *spawning* ___	ivitaaruq
cheap; *is* ___	akikittuq
cheaper; *gets it* ___	akikittuqtaarijaa
cheaper; *is* ___	akikitqijaujuq
cheat; *always* ___s	iqutujuq; haglutujuq
cheats	iqujuq; haglujuq
cheek	uluak/uludjak/uludjat)
chews	tamuqtuq
chews a skin to soften it	angulajuq
chews continuously	tamuajuq
chews it	tamuqtaa
chews it for him/her/it	tamuutijaa (*see* niripkaqtaa)
child	nutaraq (d. *nutaqqak*, pl. *nutaqqat*)
child; *adopted* ___	tiguaq
child; *gives birth to a* ___	nutaqqijuq; utaqqijuq
child; *middle* ___	akulliqun/akulliqut/akulliquti
chimney	pujurvik
chin	tablu
chin; *raises his* ___	aarluqtuq
chirps (of birds)	tiuqtiuqtuq
chisel; *ice* ___	tuuq
chisel; *works with a* ___	tuuqtuq
chisels it	tuuqtaa
chokes (while drinking)	hittuqittuq; tupittuq
Christmas	Quviahugvik
church	aturvik; angaadjuvik
cigar	higaarjuaq
cigarette	higaaq
cigarette paper	higaakhaq
circle	kaimalluriktuq
clavicle	qutuk
claw	kukik
clay	qiku

clean; *is* ___	halumajuq
clear; *is not* ___	takummarikhilimaittuq
clearing up; *the sky is* ___	allaliqtuq
cleft chin	tablurut
cliff	imnaq
climb; *uses it to* ___ *up*	tunmirarijaa
climbs up	majuaqtuq; majuraqtuq
clock	ubluqhiun/ubluqhiut/ubluqhiuti
close by	qanilrumi
close; *they (two) are* ___ *to each other*	qanikturiiktuk
closed; *is* ___	umiktuq
closes his/her/its mouth	ipummiqtuq
closes the door	ukkuaqtuq
cloth for wiping	ivgun/ivgut/ivguti
clothes	aannuraat
clothes closet	aannuraaqarvik
clothes; *men's* ___	angunnait
clothes; *takes his/her (own)* ___ *off*	aannuraangijaqtuq; uhiqtiqtuq
clothes; *women's* ___	arnannait
clothesline	paniqhidjiqturvik
clothing; *a piece of* ___	aannuraaq
clothing; *tail of* ___	aku
cloud	nuvuja
cloudberry	aqpik
cloudy; *is* ___	nuvujalaqijuq
club	anautaq
club (in a deck of cards)	algalaq
club (his/her)	anautaa
clumsy; *is* ___	qutangajuq
coal	aluaq
coal; *live* ___	auma (pl. *aumait*)
coals; *is turning to* ___*, embers*	aumaliuqtuq

coccyx	pamialluk
cod	hiurjuktuuq
coffee	kaapi/kaaffi
coffee pot	kaapiliut; kaapiliurut
coils it	kaivjaqtaa/qipitiqtaa/qiputiqtaa
cold sweat and aching bones when developing a fever	qaaliruhuktuq
cold; *becomes* ___	niglaqtuq
cold; *becomes* ___ (weather)	niglaqtiqtuq
cold; *catches a* ___	qalalaqijuq
cold; *extreme, dry* ___	iidjiraaluk
cold; *has* ___ *hands*	algaiqhijuq; algaijaqtuq
cold; *has a* ___	qalaktuq
cold; *is* ___ (not human)	qiqaujuq; niglaqtuq
cold; *is* ___ (of living things)	alappaaqtuq; qaajuqtuq
cold; *is extremely* ___ (of metal)	puvipqurnaqtuq/puvitqurnaqtuq
cold; *is very* ___ *weather*	iidjilaqijuq; qaajurnaqtuq
cold; *it's very* ___	alappaa; iidji
collarbone	qutuk
comb; *a* ___	illaijut/illaijun/illaijaut
comes	qaijuq
comes across him/her/it	paaqtaa
comes in	itiqtuq
comes off	piiqtuq
comes off/out accidentally	niujijuq
comical	iglaqtittijuq
comical; *is* ___	qituhungnaqtuq
coming here; *is* ___	hamunngauliqtuq
commands him/her/it to do something	pitqujaa
commands someone to do something	pitquijuq
commits adultery	aallatuqtuq
companion	inuuqati; aippaq

complete; *is* ___	iluittuq
computer	qaritaujaq
conceals himself/herself/itself	iiqtuqtuq
concerned; *is* ___ *about him/her/it*	ihumaalugijaa
confronts	hurjuktuq
confused; *is* ___	nalujuq
considers something	ihumaliuqtuq
construction worker	hanaji
contain; *can* ___ *a lot*	ilutujuq
contain; *can* ___ *only a small quantity*	ilukittuq
container for ice	hikuun/hikuut/hikuuti
container to hold fish	iqaluqarvik
content; *is* ___	qujajuq
cook; *a* ___	kukialuk
cooking pot (traditionally made of soapstone)	utkuhik
cooks food to eat	niqiliuqtuq; kukiujuq
cool off; *letting something hot* ___	niglaqhiqtuq
copper	kannujaq
corner	tiritquq
correct; *is* ___	ihuaqtuq
corrects it	ihuaqhijaa
cost; *how much does it* ___	qanuq; akituva
cotton: *Arctic* ___	ipirakhat; kanguujaq
cough; *catches a* ___	qalalaqijuq
cough; *has a* ___	qalaktuq
coughs	qalaktuqtuq
counts	kihittitirijuq; kihittijuq
couple; *married* ___	arnauniriik
court	apiqhuivik

cousin on father's side (same for male and female cousin)	angutiqati
cousin on mother's side (same for male and female cousin)	arnaqati
cover; *a skin used to ___ a sled*	higjaaq
cover; *top bed___ made of caribou skin*	qaaq (pl. *qadjat*) (*see* aalliniq, alvat)
covered with a skin, blanket, etc.	qipikhimajuq
covers him/her/it with a blanket	uliktaa; qipiktaa
covers himself/herself/itself with a blanket	uliktuq
co-worker	havaqati
crack in ice caused by winter wind	uiniq
crack in spring ice that remains open	ainniq
crack in winter ice that opens and then freezes	aajuraq
cranberry	kingmingnaq
crane; *sandhill ___*	tatilgaq
crawls	paamnguqtuq; paan'nguqtuq
creek	kuutiruq; kuugarjuk
crevice	qumniq
cried for so long that he/she got tired	qian'nguqtuq
cries	qulviliuqtuq; qiajuq
crime	ihuinaaqtuq
crimping ugjuk soles with his/her teeth	kiijuq
crispy; *has become ___*	qaqqulaannguqtuq
cross; *a ___*	hanningajulik
cross-eyed	nakujuq
crosses over	ikaaqtuq; itivjaaqtuq
crosses over it	ikaaqtaa
crossing	ikaaraq
crouches down	aqubliqtuq/aqublingajuq

crunches it by mouth	qaqqulaaqtaa
cry; *makes him/her/it* ___	qiamiqhuqtaa
crystals of ice (formed on boots, fishnet, sled runners, etc.)	nulaq
cup	qallun/qallut/qalluti; qaluraun/ qaluraut/qalurauti
cured; *is* ___	mamittuq
curly hair; *has* ___	iqingajuq
current; *ocean* ___	havraq
curtains	talukujaaq
custom	pitquhiq
cut off; *has been* ___	kipihimajuq
cut off a piece	avikhijuq
cute; *is* ___	ilunngunaqtuq
cutting; *is* ___ *into many pieces*	aviktuijuq
cutting; *is* ___ *meat*	avguqhijuq; avguaqhijuq
cuts him/her/it	kiliqtaa
cuts himself/herself/itself	kiliqtuq
cuts it	kipijaa
cuts it in half	aviktaa
cuts it up	avguqtaa
cuts it up for him	avguutijaa
cuts it with scissors	kivjaqtaa
cuts something	kipijuq
cuts up	avguijuq

daddy-long-legs spider	tuktuujaq
damaged; *is* ___	ahiruqtuq

damp; *is* ___	ailaqtuq
dampness	ailaq
dance; *gone to the* ___	nummagiaktuq
dance; *is drum* ___ *ing*	qilaudjaqtuq
dance; *Russian* ___	kingmiktaq
dances	numiqtuq/mumiqtuq
dangerous; *is* ___ (of ice, water, boat, plane)	nangiarnaqtuq
dangerous; *is* ___ *because it could injure someone*	qajangnaqtuq
daring; *is* ___	alguangajuq
dark; *becomes* ___	taaqhijuq
dark; *is* ___	taaqtuq
darkness	taaq
daughter	panik
daughter; *only* ___	panituaq
daughter; *step* ___	panikhaq
daughter-in-law and mother-in-law together	ukuariik
daughter-in-law of a female	ukuaq
day	ubluq
day; *long* ___	ubluqtujuq
day; *short* ___	ubluqqukhijuq
daylight; *is* ___	qaujuq
dazzled by the sun's reflection	qinngaqtuq
dazzling	qinngarnaqtuq
dead; *is* ___	tuqungajuq
dealing; *he/she is .... a deck of cards*	auttuq
debt	atugaq (pl. *atukkat*)
debts; *has* ___	atukkiqtuq
December	Ubluiqtirvia
decides	hivunikhaqhiuqtuq; ihumaliuqtuq
deep; *is* ___	itijuq
defecates	anaqtuq

delicious; *is* ___	mamaqtuq
delivery; *water ___ person*	imiqtaqti
Delta braid	qupak
demanding; *is* ___	atan'ngujaq
den; *polar bear* ___	apittaaq (*see* apittiuvik)
Dene	Itqiliq
dental instrument	kiguhiqqun/kiguhiqqut/kiguhiqquti
dented; *is* ___	tukhungajuq
dentist	kigutiliqiji; kiguhiqiji
dents it	tukhuktaa
departs	aullaqtuq
depleted; *is* ___	nunguttuq
depletes it	nungutaa
descends	hituaqtuq; anmuujuq
destination	hivuniq
detergent	irmiut/irmiun/irmiuti
devil	tupilak
diamond (in a deck of cards)	hitkik
diaper	makkaq
diaphragm in chest cavity	kanivaun/kanivaut/kanivauti
diarrhea; *has* ___	itiktaqtuq
dies	huiqtuq; tuqujuq
dies; *almost* ___	tuqutqajaktuq; tuqulrajaqtuq
different one	aalla
different; *becomes* ___	aallannguqtuq
different; *in/on/at a ___ one*	aallami
different; *is* ___	aallangajuq
different; *they (two) are* ___	aallatqiiktuk
difficult; *is* ___	nalunaqtuq; naunaqtuq; ajurnaqtuq
digs	algaktuq
digs him/her/it out	nivaktaa
dimple	itiqhaq
direction; *changes* ___	hangujuq

direction; *in which* ___	hunamun/hunamut
dirt	puja
dirt; *patches of* ___ *on bottom of lake or sea*	natirluit
dirty; *is* ___	halumaittuq
disagrees	anginngittuq; angiqhimanngittuq
disappears	talittuq
disembark; *a place to* ___	niudjivik; apurvik; tulagvik
disembark; *is allowed to* ___	atkaqtuq
disembarks from a vehicle or boat	niujuq
disgruntled	mamiahuktuq
dish cupboard	qallutiqarvik
displays it	hatqummiqtaa
distant; *the most* ___ *one*	ungalliq
distress; *is in* ___	kappiahuktuq; iqhijuq
distressing; *is* ___	kappianaqtuq; iqhinaqtuq
distributes something	aittuqtuijuq
dives repeatedly	agluraqtuq
dives under water (of animals)	agluqtuq; puuvjaqtuq
divides it	aviktaa
divides them into two piles or groups	malrunnguqtait
division	avgun
divorced; *is* ___	avittuq
divorced; *they (two) are* ___	avittuk
divorces him/her	avitaa
dizzy (from spinning around)	kaiffan'nguqtuq
do; *is looking for something to* ___	hulijakhaqhiuqtuq
do; *something to* ___	hulijakhaq
dock	niudjivik; apurvik; tulagvik
does this	taimailiuqtuq
dog	qinmiq
dog collar	qunguhiqtaun/qunguhiqtaut/qunguhiqtauti

dog dish	alugvik
dog pulls	qimuktuq
dog refuses to pull	qimujuittuq
dog team; *goes by* ___	qinmiqtuqtuq
dog team trace line	qitun'ngaq
dog; *female* ___	arnaaqutaq
dog; *last* ___ *in the team*	uniaqti
dog; *lead* ___	hivuliqti
dog; *second lead* ___	tugliqti
dog; *young* ___	qinmiarjuk
dogs; *calls the* ___	qanmaqtuq
dogs; *harnessing up the* ___	qitun'ngaqtuijuq
dogs; *has lots of* ___	qinmigiaktuq
dogs; *running the* ___	qimuktittijuq
dogs right behind the leader	qimuktik
dogs right behind the qimuktik	tugliqtik
dogs right next to the sled	uniaqtik
doing; *what are you* ___	hulivit/hulivin
doing; *what is he/she/it* ___	huliva
doll	inuujaq
door	ukkuaq
door; *closes the* ___	ukkuaqtuq
door; *opens the* ___	ukkuiqtuq
doormat	aluijarvik
doorstep	abluriq
doorway	paaq; paa
dough rises	publakhiijuq
doughnut	putuligaq
down of bird, muskox, etc.	qiviuq
down; *goes* ___	atqaqtuq
downward	anmun/anmut
drafty; *is* ___	anuqhaaqtuq
drafty; *is* ___ (indoors)	aqhaluktuq

drags	uniaqtuq
drags him/her/it	uniaqtaa
drawer	iliqpik; iliuqpik
draws	titiraujaqtuq
drawstring around top of boot	ungirun/ungirut/ungiruti
dreams	hinnaktuqtuq
dreams; *in your* ___	hinnakturni
dress	qitaujaq
dressed; *is already* ___	aannuraariiqtuq
dresses himself/herself/itself	aannuraaqtuq
dresses up	aannuraaqtuqtuq
dried fish	piffi
dries	paniqhiqtuq
drifted ashore; *anything that* ___	tivjaq
drifting snow	natiruvik
drifts away	haavittuq
driftwood	tivjat
driftwood; *fetches* ___	tivjaqtaqtuq
drill	ikuutaq
drill bits	ikuutautit
drill; *wood* ___	pukkuliqhit
drills	ikuutaqtuq
drinking broth to produce milk	amaamakhaliuqtuq
drinks	imiqtuq; -tuq-; niuqqaqtuq; niuqhijuq
drinks it	imiqtaa
drips	kuhiqtuq
drips repeatedly	kuhiqtaqtuq
driver	aquti
drives a vehicle/boat	aquttuq
drizzle	miniq
drizzles	minilaqijuq
droll; *is* ___	qituhungnaqtuq
dropped off; *is* ___	atkaqtuq

drops	ijukkaqtuq
drops by on his/her way	apquhaaqtaa
drops him/her/it	kataktaa
drops something	kataijuq
drowns	immittuq
drum (container)	qattarjuk; qattarjuaq
drum (musical instrument)	qilaun/qilaut/qilauti
drum; *beats the* ___	katuktuq
drum dance song	pihiq
drum dance; *does a* ___	qilaudjaqtuq
drumstick	katuun/katuut/katuuti
drunk; *is* ___	imingajuq
dry; *is* ___	paniqtuq
drying rack	paniqhiivik
drying rack for fish or meat	qimirutit
duck; *female king eider* ___	mitiq (*see* hurluqtuuq)
duck; *female common eider* ___	hurluqtuuq (*see* mitiq)
duck; *"It's only a female king eider* ___*" (expression)*	mitiinnaq
duck; *male common eider* ___	amaulik
duck; *king eider* ___	qingalik
duffle; *long* ___ *sock*	aliqti (d. *aliqtik*)
duck; *long-tailed* ___	aahanngiq
duffle; *short* ___ *sock*	piniraq
dull; *it is* ___	ipiiqtuq
dumb; *is* ___	qaujimaittuq
dust	ihiq
dust or snow is blowing behind a moving vehicle	natiruvilaqutijuq
dwarf	inuarullik
dwarf birch	uqpik (*see* avaalaqiaq)

E

eagle	qupanuaqpak
eagle; golden ____	tingmiaqpak; qupanuaqpak
ear	hiun/hiut/hiuti (d. *hiutik*)
earache; *has an* ____	hiulliuqtuq; hiulluktuq
east wind	nigiq
east; *wind is blowing from the* ____	nigiqtuq
eastward	kivanmun/kivanmut
easy; *is* ____ *to do*	pijuminaqtuq
eat; *gets him/her/it something to* ____	niqikhaqtaa
eats	nirijuq; -tuq
eats it	nirijaa
echoes more than once	imiarjiraqtuq
echoes once	imiaqtuq; imiarjijuq
edge (of lake, sea, river)	hinaa
edge; *at its* ____	kiglingani
edge; *at the* ____ *of sea, river or lake*	hinaani
edge; *cutting* ____ *of knife, axe*	ipikharniq
edge; *goes along the* ____	hinaaguuqtuq
edge; *sharp* ____	quagjuk
effort; *makes an* ____	akhuuqtuq
effort; *use more* ____	akhun
egg	mannik (pl. *manniit*)
egg; *(bird) lays an* ____	manniliuqtuq
eggs; *fish* ____	huvak
eggs; *sits on its* ____	itquqtuq
eggs; *takes the* ____ *out of a fish*	huvaiqtuq
eggshell	hauniq
eh	ai

eight	arvinilik malruk
elbow	ikuhiq
elbow; *hurts his/her/its* ___	ikuttiaqtuq
elbow; *leans on his/her* ___	ikuhingmingaaqtuq
elbow; *pokes him/her/it with his/her* ___	ikuhingmiktaa
elbows	ikuhik
Elder	inirnikhaaq; inutuqaq
eldest sibling	angajukhiqun
electrician	alruhiqiji
else; *mistook him/her/it for someone/something* ___	aallaunahugijaa
else; *somewhere* ___	ahiani; ahini
elsewhere	ahiani; ahini
ember	auma (pl. aumait)
embers; *is turning to* ___ *or coals*	aumaliuqtuq
emptied; *has been* ___	imaiqtuq
empties it	imaiqtaa
empty; *is* ___	imaittuq
end	kigliq
end; *at the* ___ *of it*	ihuani
end; *at the* ___ *of something about to be finished or depleted*	nunguani
English language	Qablunaatun/Qablunaatut
enjoyable; *is* ___	alianaqtuq
enough; *has had* ___ *of it*	ariujaa
enough; *is* ___	naammaktuq
enough; *that's* ___	taimak
enters	itiqtuq
entrance	paaq; paa
envious; *is* ___	tuhujuq
envious; *is* ___ *of him/her/it*	tuhugijaa
envious; *is always* ___	tuhutujuq
epidermis	uvinik

escapes	annaktuq
European-style dance	hukkijaaqtuq
evening	unnuk
examines it	ihivriuqtaa
exchanges it	himmauhiqtaa
excrement	anaq
exhausted; *is* ___	tungullaktuq
expecting to meet him/her/it	inukhiarijaa
expensive; *is* ___	akitujuq
expensive; *is too* ___	akituvallaaqtuq
explains to him/her/it	hivuniqhipkaqtaa
extends it	takhijaa
extinguished; *is* ___ (of fire)	qamittuq
extinguisher; *fire* ___	qaptirun
extremity; *at its* ___	ihuani
eye	iji
eye; *has sore* ___	ijarluktuq
eye; *hurts his/her/its* ___	ijaruqtuq
eye; *pupil of the* ___	ijaruvak
eyebrow	qablu
eyebrows; *knits his/her* ___	qinngurluktuq
eyeglasses	ilgaak/ilgak
eyelash	qimiriaq
eyelid	tunujaq
eyes; *closes his/her* ___	hikunngiqtuq/hikunngiqtuq/ hikunriqtuq
eyes; *half opens her/its/his* ___	uitapqaqtuq
eyes; *has his/her/its* ___ *open*	uitajuq
eyes; *opens his* ___	uittuq
eyes; *pair of* ___	ijik
eyesight (has poor eyesight)	iigluktuq

face	kiinaq; akuliak/akuliaq
face; *has a nice* ___	akuliariktuq
faces someone/something	haattuq; hanmijuq
facing each other	hanmitijuk
fact; *in* ___	taimaa
faith; *has true* ___	pitquhiqtujuq
faith; *strong* ___	pitquhiqtujuq
faithful	pitquhiqtujuq
falcon; *peregrine*	kilgavik
fall	ukiaq
fall; *early* ___	ukiakhaq
falls	ijukkaqtuq; ulrujuq
falls backward	niviqtuq
falls flat on his/her face	pallukaqtuq
falls into water	imaaqtuq
falls through (ice, floor, etc.)	nakkaqtuq
falls with a crash	affaqpallaijuq
familiar; *looks* ___	ilitarnaqtuq
far; *are equally* ___ *apart*	ungahikkutigiiktut
far; *is* ___ *away*	ungahiktuq
farther; *gets* ___ *away*	ungahikhijuq
farther; *is* ___ *away*	ungahiaqtuq
farthest out at sea	kiilliq
farthest; *the* ___ *one*	ungalliq
farthest; *the one* ___ *away*	ungahitqijaq; avalliq
farthest; *the one* ___ *behind*	tunulliq
farts	niliqtuq
fast; *is* ___	kajumiktuq
fat on kidneys	taqturun/taqturut/taqturuti

INUINNAQTUN TO ENGLISH

fat on top of broth	puiniq (*see* qaluiraqtuq)
fat; *is a ___ person*	puvalajuq
fat; *takes the ___ off top of broth*	qaluiraqtuq (*see* puiniq)
father	aappak; paapak
father-in-law (or mother-in-law)	haki
father-in-law and mother-in-law	hakiak
feather	huluk; mitquq (pl. *mitquit*); qiviuq
feather; *long ___ of tail or wing*	huluk
feathers; *has no more ___, fur, or hair*	mitquiqtuq
February	Iidjirurvia
fed up with him/her/it	ariujaa
feeds him/her/it	niripkaqtaa
feeling	ikpiguhungniq; ikpingnarniq
feet are turned in	kuungajuq
female animal	arnalluq
fence; *___ that surrounds an area*	haputaq avataagut
fetches something	aikhiqtuq; -taq-; -tauti
fetches something for him/her/it	aikhiutijaa
fever	kidjak
fever; *developed a ___*	kidjalaqijuq
fever; *has a ___*	kidjaktuq
few	ikittut
fiddle	agiraq; uluaraut
fiddle; *plays ___*	uluaraqtuq; agiraqtuq
fight each other	ningaqtut
fighting a war; *are ___*	angujaktut
fights back	akiraqtuqtuq
fights; *a child ___*	unuqtuq
file	agiaq
files it	agiaqtaa
files something	agiaqtuq
filled; *is ___ up to overflowing*	ulipkaaqtuq

fillet (of meat)	uliuhiniq
filling it up	tatatirijuq
fills it	immiqtaa
fills it up	tatattaa
fills it up to overflowing	ulipkaaqtaa
fills it up to the brim	tatatpiaqtaa
finds him/her/it	nanijaa
finds it by chance	nalvaaqtaa
fine; *is* ___	qanurinngittuq; naammaktuq
finger	inugaq (pl. *inukkat*)
finger; *index* ___	tikiq
finger; *little* ___	iqitquq
finger; *middle* ___	qitiqhiq
finger; *ring* ___	mikiliraq
fingernail	kukik
fingertip; *end of* ___ (mainly of thumb and index finger)	puudjuk
finished; *is* ___	iniqtuq
finishes it up	nungutaa
fire	ingniq
fire; *is on* ___	ikittuq
fire; *lights a* ___	ikittijuq
fire; *sets* ___ *to him/her/it*	ikipkaqtaa
fire; *something to light* ___ *with*	ikuallautikhaq; ikkitautikhaq
fire; *they are on* ___	ikittut
fireplace made with rocks	kikhugvik
fires a gun	hiquriaqtuq
fires at him/her/it	hiquriaqtaa
fire starter	ikkitautikhaq; ikuallautikhaq
firing pin of gun	qagaqtaut/qagaqtaun
first of all	hivullirmik
first; *is the* ___	hivulliujuq
first; *the* ___ *one*	hivulliq

First Nations person	Itqiliq
fiscal year	maniqautit ukiunga
fish eggs	huvak
fish guts	hunagait
fish heads; *aged* ___	qaqquq
fish heads; *cooked* ___	patau
fish heads; *cooks* ___	patauliuqtuq
fish of salmonid family (char, trout, etc.)	iqaluk
fish; *catches a* ___	iqaluktuq
fish; *dried* ___	piffi
fish; *eats cooked* ___ *heads*	patautuqtuq (*see* qaqquqtuqtuq)
fish; *eats gamy* ___ *heads*	qaqquqtuqtuq (*see* patautuqtuq)
fish; *frozen* ___ *or meat*	quaq
fish; *they get lots of* ___	iqalliqijut
fishing line	uipkuaq
fishing rod	iqalukhiun/iqalukhiut (*also* iqqaqhaut)
fishing spear	kakivak; nuijaaqpak
fishing; *is* ___	iqalukhiuqtuq
fishing; *is going* ___	iqalliaqtuq
fishnet	kuvjaq
fishnet; *catches it in a* ___	kuvjaqtaa
fishnet; *checks a* ___	kuvjaqhuqtuq
fishnet; *sets a* ___	kuvjaqtuqtuq; kuvjiqtuq; kuvjiqhijuq
fishweir	hapun/haput/haputi
fist	tigluun/tigluut/tigluuti
fist; *hits him/her/it with a* ___	tigluktaa
fits just right	nalaumajuq
five	tallimat
fixes	hanajuq
fixes it	hanajaa; ihuaqhijaa
flame	ikumaniq
flammable; *is* ___	ikittaaqtuq

flashlight	naniruun/naniruut/naniruuti
flat land	natirnaq
flat; *is* ___	naqittuq; attariktuq
flavour; *has no* ___	iptiittuq
flavour; *has no more* ___	iptiiqtuq
flew away (bird, insect)	tingijuq
flexible	pirittaaqtuq
flies	tingmijuq; tingittuq
flies away	tingmikhajuq
flintstone	ingak; ingnikhaq
flipper; *front* ___ *of a seal*	taliruq
flipper; *seal's rear* ___	hiitquq
float	puptan/puptat/puptati
floats	puptajuq
floor	natiq
flour	muqpaujaq
flower	nauttiaq
flows	maqijuq
fly	niviuvak
fly; *small* ___	niviuvarjuk
fly away; *starting to* ___	tingitiqtuq
foam	qapuk
fog	taktuk; takhiq (*see* quunilaqijuq)
fog; *there is ice* ___	quunilaqijuq (*see* takhiqtuq, taktuktuq)
foggy; *is* ___	takhiqtuq; taktuktuq (*see* quunilaqijuq)
foggy; *very* ___	taktugaaluk
follows behind	mallaujuq
follows behind him/her/it	maliktaa
food	niqi
food; *makes* ___ *to eat*	niqiliuqtuq; kukiujuq
food; *sweet* ___	hiirnaqtuq
foot	itigak

foot; *kicks it with his/her* ___	tukkaqtaa
football; *plays* ___	aqhaktuq
footprint	tumi
forehead	qauq
foreigner	tuurmiaq
forest fire; *smoke from a* ___	ihiriaq
forever	nungulaittumun/nungulaittumut; taimunga
forgets	puiguqtuq
forgets him/her/it	puiguqtaa
foster child	haimmiqut
foster parent	haimmiqiji
foster parenting	haimmiqijuq
fork	kapuraun/kapuraut/kapurauti
formerly	ingilraan
found it	nanihijuq
four	hitamat
fowl	tingmiaq
fox; *blue* ___	qian'ngaqtaq
fox; *cross* ___	kiahirutilik
fox; *red* ___	kajuqtuq
fox; *white* ___	tiriganniaq
frame; *tent* ___	qanaik
framing; *construction* ___	qanaktaq
free; *gets them for* ___	akiittuqtaqtuq
free; *is* ___	akiittuq
freezer	quaqarvik; qiqittiivi
freezes	qiqijuq
Friday	Tallimmiut
friend	ilannaq
friend; *special* ___	iviurnauti
friends; *two* ___	ilannariik
frightened; *is* ___	iqhijuq; kappiahuktuq

frightened; *is ___ by him/her/it*	iqhigijaa; kappiagijaa
frightening; *is ___*	iqhinaqtuq; kappianaqtuq
from me	uvamnit
from where	humit/humin
from; *where are you ___*	humiutauvit/humiutauvin
from; *where did you come ___*	nakit qaivit
from; *where did you get it ___*	nakin pijat
front	hivuniq
front part of something	hivu
front; *in ___ of him/her/it*	hivuani
frost formed inside the house	ilu
frosted on the inside	patuktuq
frowning	qaqhuliqijuq
frowns	qinngurluktuq
frozen cheeks; *has ___*	uluadjaktuq
fruit	ahiaq; paunraq
fruit; *gathers ___*	ahiaqtaqtuq; paun'ngaqtaqtuq
frying pan	hiratittit; hiqanakhiut/hiqanakhiun/ hiqanakhiuti; haqanakhiut (*see* ipualik)
fuel delivery person	uqhurjualiqiji
fuel oil	uqhurjuaq
fuel tank	uqhuqarvik
fuel truck	uqhurjuaqtaun/uqhurjuaptaut/ uqhurjuaqtauti; uqhurjuaqtaut
full; *is ___*	tatattuq
full; *is ___ after eating*	aqiattuqtuq
full; *it is ___ of people*	inugiaktuq
full; *still feels ___*	aqiattuhuktuq
fun; *is ___*	alianaqtuq
funding sources	maniqautit
funny; *is ___*	qituhungnaqtuq
funny; *is not ___*	alianaittuq
fur	mitquq (pl. *mitquit*)

fur; *has no more* ___, *hair, or feathers*	mitquiqtuq
fur nipple protector (for breastfeeding dogs, to prevent freezing)	muluilitaq
fur trim on a parka	qalviqut
furnace	uqquuqun; uunaqun
future	hivuniq
future; *to the* ___	hivumun/hivumut

G

gains weight	puvallaqtuq
gall bladder	hungaq
game animal	anngun/anngut/annguti; nirjun/nirjut/nirjuti
game; *are playing skin toss, blanket toss* ___	avataaqtaqtu
game; *card* ___	piannauhiq
game; *got a* ___ *animal*	angujuq
game; *hunts small* ___	huraaqhiuqtuq
game; *plays string* ___ *s*	ajaraaqtuq
game; *plays the arm pulling* ___	aqamaaktuq
game; *string* ___	ajaraaq
garbage	iqqakuuq
garbage can/bin	iqqakuurvik
garbage collector	iqqakuuqti
garbage truck	iqqakuurun/iqqakuurut/iqqakuuruti
gas; *has* ___ (a human)	publaktuq
gathered; *are* ___	katittut
gathers something	katitirijuq

get; *goes to* ___ *him/her/it*	aijaa; -taq-; -tauti-; aikhiqtu
get off; *a place to* ___	niudjivik; apurvik; tulagvi
gets a game animal	angujuq
gets out of a vehicle or boat	niujuq
gets up (from prone or sitting position)	makittuq
gets up (from sleeping)	tupaktuq
getting out of waves	qainniqijuq
giant	inukpagjuaq/inukpak
gift; *a* ___ *given*	aittuun/aittuut/aittuuti
gift; *a received* ___	aittuuhiaq
gift; *gives a* ___	aittuqtuq
gift; *gives him/her/it a* ___	aittuqtaa
gift; *gives it as a* ___	aittuutigijaa
gift; *receives a* ___	aittuuhiaqtuq
gills (of a fish)	mahik
girl; *teenaged* ___	arnaruhiq
give it to me	qaidjuk
gives away	aittuqtuq
gives it	tunijaa
gives it as a present	aittuutigijaa
gives something	tunihijuq
glass	hikuliaq
glass; *drinking* ___	imngun, inmgut (*also* imngum/ imngut)
glove	algaaq (d. *algaak*)
gloves; *a pair of* ___	algaak
glue	nipitirun/nipitirut/nipitiruti
gnaws; *an animal* ___	kigiqtuq (*see* kigaqtuq)
gnaws it	kipkaqtaa
gnaws; *a human* ___	kipkaqtuq (*see* kigiqtuq)
go; *let's* ___	taki
God	ataniq
goes down	anmuujuq; hituaqtuq

goes out	anijuq
goes to see him/her/it	upaktaa
goes up	qunmuujuq; qunmuktuq
goes uphill	majuraqtuq/majuaqtuq
gone; *has been ___ for a long time*	aullaqhimakhaaqtuq
good fishing place (Cambridge Bay)	iqaluktuuttiaq (Iqaluktuuttiaq)
good; *is ___*	nakuujuq
goose; *Canada ___*	uluagullik
goose; *snow*	kanguq
goose; *white-fronted ___*	nirlivik
gores him/her/it with antlers or horns	nagjungmiktaa
gossips	unnirluktuq
got it; *recently ___*	pihaaqtaa
grabbed; *is ___*	aqhaaqtaujuq
grandchild	in'ngutaq/irngutaq
grandfather	ataattiaq
grandmother	anaanattiaq
grass; *blade of ___*	ivik (pl. ivgit)
grasshopper	pigliriaq
grateful; *is ___*	qujahuktuq
grave	iluviq (d. *iluviik*, pl. *iluvrit*)
gravel	ujaraliaq
graveyard	iluviqhivik
grazes	niriniaqtuq
grazes him/her/it	kahakaffuktaa
great-grandfather	ataatattiaq
greedy; *is ___*	uningajuq
green	hungajaaqtuq
greenish-yellow	hungajangajuq
grey	qirnarraaqtuq
grey/white hair on human	qiiq
growls	qatiggaaqtuq

grows	angiglijuq
grumbles	uqamaluktuq
gull; *glaucous* ___	naujaq
gull; *Sabine's* ___	iqalgagiaq; iqilgagiaq
gum (of the mouth)	itkiq
gum; *chewing* ___	kuttuq
gun	hiqquut/hiqquun/hiqquqtidjun/ hiqquqtidjut/hiqquqtiun/ hiqquqtidjuti
gun powder	arjakhaq
gun shell; *empty* ___	kinguniq
gun; *aims at something with a* ___ (or other object)	kijuaqtuqtuq
gun; *fires a* ___	hiquriaqtuq
gun; *firing pin of a* ___	qagaqtaut/qagaqtaun
gun; *shoots at him/her/it with a* ___	hiquriaqtaa
gun; *shoots it/him/her with a* ___	hiquqtaa
guts a fish/game animal	hunagaijaijuq; aqiaruijaijuq
guts it	aqiaruijaqtaa
gyrfalcon	kilgavikpak

habit	pitquhiq
hacksaw	havviqun
haemorrhaging	adjijuq
hair on the head	nujaq (pl. *nujait*)
hair; *grey/white* ___ *on a young person*	nutiblik
hair; *grey/white* ___ *on human*	qiiq

hair; *has long, shaggy* ___	tulrujuq
hair; *has lots of grey/white* ___	qidjaktuq
hair; *has messy* ___	nujarluktuq
hair; *has no* ___	nujaittuq
hair; *has no more* ___	nujaiqtuq
hair; *has no more* ___, *fur, or feathers*	mitquiqtuq
hair; *has short* ___ (of animals)	mitqukittuq
hair; *human body* ___	mitquq (pl. mitquit) (*see* nujaq, tingiq, huluk)
hair; *pubic* ___	tingiq
hair; *scrapes the* ___ *or fur off a hide*	mitquiqtaa
half; *cuts it in* ___	aviktaa
hall; *meeting* ___	katimavik (*see* katilvik)
hammer	kautaujaq
hand	algak (d. *algaak*)
hand it over	qaidjuk
hand; *holds his/her* ___	tahiuqtaa
hand; *palm of* ___	itimak
hand; *shakes* ___s *with*	aatituuqtuq
hand; *side of* ___	arvak
hand; *uses only one* ___	iglupiaqtuqtuq
handle	ipu
hands; *has cold* ___	algaijaqtuq; algaiqhijuq
hands; *uses both* ___	igluktuqtuq
handwriting	titirauhiq
hanger	nivinngarvik
hangs it up (on a wall)	nivinngaqtaa
happy; *is* ___	aliahuktuq; quviahuktu
happy; *is always* ___	quviahuujuq
hard; *is* ___ *to understand*	nalunaqtuq/naunaqtuq
hare	ukaliq

hare; *young* ___	ukalaaq
harness	anu *(d. annuk,* pl. *annut)*
harnessed a dog	anuhijuq
harnesses it	anujaa
harpoon	kapuun/kapuut/kapuuti
harpoon for throwing	nauligaq
harpoon head	naulaq
harpoon shaft	unaaq
harpoons it	nauliktaa
hat	naharaq; nahaq; titqiaq
hawk	qupanuaqpak
hazy; *is* ___	takummarikhilimaittuq
head; *keeps his* ___ *up*	aarlungajuq
head; *put his* ___ *back*	aarluqtuq
head; *shakes his* ___ *to say no*	niaqqulrujuq *(see* imannaaqtuq, qinngijuq)
head; *something is wrong in the* ___	niaqurluktuq
headache; *has a* ___	niaqurliuqtuq; niaqunngujuq
headwind	algu
health; *good* ___	pimattiarniq; aanniaqtailiniq
hearing; *has good* ___	hiudjariktuq
hearing; *is hard of* ___	hiudjarluktuq
hears (a continuous sound)	tuhaajuq
hears (a short sound)	tuhaqtuq
hears him/her/it (continuous sound)	tuhaajaa
hears him/her/it (short sound)	tuhaqtaa
heart	uumman/uummat/uummati
heart (in a deck of cards)	iqquk (d. *iqquuk)*
heart; *main* ___ *artery*	qaalluviaq
heater	uqquuqun/uqquuqut/uqquuquti
heather; *Arctic* ___	ikhun/ikhut/ikhuti
heather; *Arctic* ___ *used to start a fire*	kikhuutit *(see* ikhun)

heaven	qilak
heavy; *is* ___	uqumaittuq
heel	kingmitquq
hello; *says* ___	aatituuqtuq; haluuqtuq
helped; *it can't be* ___	ajurnarman/ajurnarmat
helper	ikajuqti
helps	ikajuqtuq
helps him/her/it	ikajuqtaa
here	hamani; hamna
here he/she/it is	uvva
here; *is* ___	ittuq
here; *is coming* ___	hamunngauliqtuq
here; *not* ___	huittuq
here; *people from* ___	hamanirmiut
here; *these right* ___	hamma
here; *this one* ___	una
hesitant (to look at people)	ilirahuuq
hibernates	apittiujuq
hibernation place	apittiuvik; apittaaq
hiccups; *has the* ___	nigituraqtuq
hide; *animal* ___	amiq (d. *ammak*, pl. *amrit*)
hides	iiqtuq; takuttailijuq; talittuq
hides him/her/it	iiqtaa
hides himself/herself/itself	iiqtuqtuq
hid something	iiqhijuq
hip bone	hilviaq
hip bones	qujapikkak
hip waders	ipirautik
hits him/her/it with fist	tigluktaa
hoarfrost	patuk
hold; *can* ___ *only a small quantity*	ilukittuq
hold; *can* ___ *a lot*	ilutujuq
holds his/her hand	tahiuqtaa

holds it	tigummijaa
hole	pakkaq
hole to pass rope through on a sled	pukkuk
hole; *fishing* ___	agluaq
hole; *makes a fishing* ___	aglualiuqtuq
hole; *natural or human-made* ___ *through ice*	pittaq
hole; *natural or human-made* ___ *through something*	putu
hole; *seal's breathing* ___	aglu
hole; *waits at a seal's breathing* ___	nippaqtuq/nikpaqtuq
home	angilrarvik
home; *goes* ___	aijuq; angilraujuq
home; *hasn't gone* ___	ainngittuq
home; *is back* ___	angilraqtuq
home; *is on the way* ___	angilrauliqtuq
home; *stays* ___ *while the others are going out*	paijuq
homebrew	immiugaq
homebrew; *makes* ___	immiuqtuq
homesick	aihiqtuq; angilraqhiqtuq
homeward; *heading* ___	utimuujuq/utimuuqtuq
hood; *parka* ___	nahaq (*see* naharaq)
hood; *tip of parka* ___	kaavjiq
hook	nivinngarvik
hook; *fish* ___	nikhik
hooks it	nikhiktaa
horn	nagjuk
horse	qinmiqpak
hospital	aanniarvik
hot; *is* ___	aumaallaktuq; uunaqtuq
house	iglu
house; *his/her* ___	iglua
house builder	igluliuqti

house maintenance person	igluliqiji
how	qanuq
how are you (singular)	qanuritpit/qanuritpin
how do you say it	qanuq taivakpiuk
how is he/she/it	qanuritp
how many	qaffit
how old are you	qaffinik ukiuqaqqit/qaffinik ukiuqaqqin
how old is he/she/it	qaffinik ukiuqaqqa/ukiuqaaqqa
howling	murruuqtuq
howls with pain	maraaqtuq
hugs him/her/it	iqitaa
hummock	angiptak
hums	ingmiqtuq
hungry; is ___	kaaktuq
hunt; comes back empty-handed from ___ing or fishing	hunamiaqtuq
hunt; she/he told me to go walking on the sea ice to ___ seals	atiqujaanga
hunter	angunahuaqti; anguniaqti
hunter on ice	tuvaaq (pl. tuvirrat)
hunter; is a skilled ___	anguhuqtuq
hunts	angunahuaqtuq; anguniaqtuq
hunts around by foot	aavaqtuq
hunts seals by foot on the ice (with dogs)	atiqtuq
hunts small game	huraaqhiuqtuq
hurries	qilamiuqtuq
hurry up	qilamik
hurts himself/herself/itself	aanniqtuq
hurts the foot through sole of soft boots	tuudjaarnaqtuq
husband	ui/uik
hymn	atuut/atuun/atuuti

I	uvanga
ice (on a pond, lake, or ocean)	hiku
ice bridge on the sea ice	pilagiaq
ice cream; *Inuit* ___	akutaq
ice floe; *landfast* ___	tuvak
ice is forming	hikuaqtuq
ice piles up	ivujuq/ivuuqtuq
ice; *candle* ___	illaujaq
ice; *crystal* ___ **(formed on boots, fishnet, sled runners, etc.)**	nulaq
ice; *melts* ___ *or snow to make water*	immiuqtuq
ice; *open lead in* ___ *created by winter wind*	uiniq
ice; *patches of rough* ___	maniillat
ice; *recently formed* ___	hikulihaaq
ice; *rough* ___	maniilaq
ice; *young* ___	hikuaqtuq
iceberg	piqalujaq
icicle	hikuarniq; qurlurniq; kuhirniq
identical; *they (two) are* ___	aadjigiiktuk/aadjikkiiktuk
imitates him/her/it	idjuaqtaa/igjuaqtaa
impact	ikpingnarniq; ikpiguhungniq
impatient; *is always* ___	palvitujuq
important	ikpingnaqtuq
impossible; *it's* ___	ajurnarman/ajurnarmat
incapable; *is* ___	ajuqtuq
incorrect; *is* ___	ihuittuq
independent; *is* ___	ilikkuurujuq; ilikkuuqtuq
independent; *is consistently* ___	ilikkuurujuktuq

indistinct; *is* ___	takummarikhilimaittuq
inexpensive; *is* ___	akikittuq
inflated; *is* ___	puviqhimajuq
inhaled	hiluqhijuq
injection; *gives him/her/it an* ___	kapijaa
inland; *goes farther* ___	tigvaqtuq
innermost	ilulliq
inside of it	iluani
inside out	ulin'ngajuq
instrument; ___ *to cut something*	avgun/avgut
inside; *bring it* ___	itiruk
inside; *has nothing* ___	iluliittuq
inside; *has something* ___	ilulilik
inside; *the* ___	ilua
inside; *the one* ___	tatqamna
inside; *to the* ___ *of that one*	tatqamunga
intelligent	ihumatujuq
intelligent; *is* ___	pilgujuq
interested; *are* ___ *in each other*	hanmitijuk
interpreter	numiktiriji
interprets	numiktirijuq
intimidated; *always* ___ *or scared*	ilirahuuq/ilarahuktuq/ilirahuktuq
intimidated; *is* ___	ilirahuktuq/ilarahuktuq
intimidating; *is* ___	ilaranaqtuq; iliranaqtuq
Inuit; *an* _____ *person*	Inuinnaq
Inuit; *in the* _____ *language*	Inuinnaqtun
invalid; *is an* ___	aqtuliqtuq
invisible; *is* ___	takunnaittuq
iris	qulvikhaq
iron (metal)	havihuk
iron; *soldering* ___	auktirun/auktirut/auktiruti
island	qikiqtaq
itch; *scratches an* ___	kumiktuq
itchy; *is* ___	kukuktuq

J

jackknife	ukutitaq
jaeger (bird); *Arctic* ___ (*also* skua)	ihunngaq
January	Ubluqtuhinia
jawbone	agliruq
jealous; *is* ___	hangiaktuq (*also* hain'ngihuktuq/ hain'riguhuktuq; hain'ngiguhuktuq; hain'ngijuq)
jellyfish	nuvilhaq
jigging rod (for jigging fish)	auladjun/auladjut/aulattidjut
jigs for fish	aulattijuq
judge of a court	apiqhuiji
judges for quality	ihivriuqhijuq
juggles	nagluqitaqtuq
juice	juus
July	Taaqhivalirvia
jumps in the air	mihiktuq
jumps once	qigliktuq; qilgiqtuq
jumps over	mihiktuq
jumps repeatedly	qigliktaqtuq; qilgiqtaqtuq
jumps with its hind legs (of caribou)	qigliriaqtuq; qilgiriaqtuq
jumpsuit (also added on)	atajuq
June	Imaruqtirvia

INUINNAQTUN TO ENGLISH

kayak	qajaq
key	kii; kiluuttaq
kicking	tukkaqtuq
kicking; *person* ____	tukkaliqtuq
kicks a dying animal	tukkaliqtuq
kicks him/her/it	itingmiktaa
kidney	taqtu (d. *taqtuk*)
kidney; *fat on* ____	taqturut/taqturun/taqturuti
killed; *is* ____	inuaqtaujuq; tuqutaujuq
kills him/her/it	inuaqtaa; tuqutaa
kills someone/something	tuquttijuq; inuaqtuq
kind; *is* ____	iliranaittuq/ilaranaittuq; palviittuq
kisses	kuniktuq
kisses him/her/it	kuniktaa
kneads dough	akuttijuq
knee	hiitquq
knee; *hurts his/her/its* ____	hiitquaqtuq
kneecap	hiitquaq
kneeling; *is* ____	hiitqumingajuq
kneels	hiitquqtuq
knife	havik
knife; *butchering* ____	pilaun/pilaut/pilauti
knife; *butter* ____	pataliqhit/pataliqhin
knife; *table* ____	nirrit (pl. nirritit)
knife; *woman's* ____	ulu
knits	nuviqhaqtuq
knitted or woven item	nuviqhaaq
knot (as in rope)	qilirniq
knot in wood	qilluq

knots it	qilirniqtaa
know; *does not* ___	ilihimanngittuq
know; *does not* ___ *what to do*	nalujuq
know; *does not* ___ *him/her/it*	nalujaa
know; *I* ___ *him/her/it*	ilihimajara
know; *I do not* ___ *why*	nauna; huukiaq
knowledge	hila
knowledgeable; *a very* ___ *person*	kapiittuq
knows *(how)*	ilihimajuq
krill	kinguq

lace for shoe or boot	hingiq
ladder	majurautaq/majuraun
ladder; *rung of a* ___	majuraun/majurautaq
ladle	qaluraun/qaluraut/qalurauti
laid down on tummy	palluqtuq
lake	tahiqn (d. *tattik, tattiit*)
lake; *small* ___	tahiraq; tahinnuaq
lamp; *traditional Inuit* ___	qulliq
land	nuna
land; *flat* ___	natirnaq
land; *looks for a place to* ___ (a boat)	apurvikhaqhiuqtuq
land; *piece of* ___ *connecting peninsula to mainland*	pituutaq
land; *point of* ___	hingik
landing place	niudjivik; apurvik; tulagvik
landing strip	mivvik/milvik

lands slowly	mittaqtuqtuq; millalauqtuq
lands; *a boat* ___	apuqtuq; tulaktuq (*see* mittuq)
lands; *plane or bird* ___	mittuq (*see* apuqtuq, tulaktuq)
landslide	akhaarniq
language	uqauhiq
language; *English* ___	Qablunaatun/Qablunaatut
language; *Inuit* ___ (of the Inuinnait)	Inuinnaqtun
lark; *horned* ___	qupanuaqpaarjuk
last time	kingullirmi
last; *the* ___ *one*	kingulliq
later	uvattiagu (*see* hadjagu/tadjagu)
later on today/tonight	ublaigumi
later; *see you* ___	uvattiaguttauq; qakuguttauq; ilaanilu; ilaanittauq
laugh; *makes people* ___	iglaqtittijuq
laugh; *try to make each other* ___	annudjutijut
laughing; *feels like* ___	qituhuktuq
laughs	iglaqtuq
laughs at him/her/it	iglautigijaa
launches it (a boat)	haavitaa
laundry; *dirty* ___	uaqtakhat
laxative	anarnaut
lazy; *is* ___	iqiahuktuq
lazy; *is habitually* ___	iqiahuujuq
lead; *open* ___ *in ice caused by winter wind*	uiniq
leaf	uqaujaq; atungaujaq
leaf tea	tiirluk
leaf; *willow* ___	atungaujaq; uqaujaq
leaks	maqijuq; inngaqtuq
lean; *a place to* ___ *one's elbows*	ajapqumiarvik
learner	kapuittuq
learns	ilihaqtuq

learns fast	ilihimmariktuq
learns from him/her/it	iliharvigijaa
learns it	ilihaqtaa
leather	qihik
leather; *made of* ___	qihigalik
leaves	aullaqtuq
leaves a group	avittuq
leeward; *on the* ___ *side*	uqquani
leeward; *the* ___ *side of a hill*	uqquaq
left over; *pieces* ___	amiakkut
left side	haumik
left; *nothing* ___	nunguttuq
left; *on his/her/its* ___	haumimni
left; *on my* ___	haumimni
left; *on your* ___	haumingni
left-handed	haumingmuuqtuq
leftover	ilakuq (pl. *ilakuit*)/amikuq
leg	niu/niuk
leg; *calf of* ___	nakahungnaq
leg; *thigh of* ___	qukturaq (d. *quqtuqqak*)
legend	unipkaaq
lemming	avin'ngaq
lends to him/her/it	atuqtitaa
lengthwise	takimun/takimut
let off; *is* ___ (from a vehicle or boat)	atkaqtuq
lets him/her/it off a boat, out of a vehicle	niudjijuq
letter (character)	titiraq (pl. *titiqqat*)
letter for someone	titirakhaq
letters	titiqqat
lever	ipigaun
library	makpiraaqarvik; taiguaqarvik
licks him/her/it once	aluktaa

licks him/her/it repeatedly	aluktuqtaa
licks once	aluktuq
licks repeatedly	aluktuqtuq
lie; *tells a ___*	iqujuq; haglujuq
lie; *that's a ___!*	iqquuk
lifts him/her/it up	kiviktaa
light; *is ___ weight*	uqittuq
light; *something to ___ a fire with*	ikuallautikhaq; ikkitautikhaq
light bulb	qulliujaq
light bulb for flashlight	qulvikhaq
lightning	ikumajaaq; qilluqiqtuq
lights a fire	ikittijuq
lights it	ikitaa
like that	taimaatun
like this	imaa; imaatun
like; *does not ___ him/her/it*	nakuuginngitaa
like; *does not ___ him/her/it very much*	nakuugilluanngita
likes him/her/it	nakuugijaa
limps	pihudjarluktuq
line; *fishing ___*	uipkuaq
line; *tump ___*	kakautaq
lip; *lower ___*	qaqhuk
lip; *upper ___ and groove under nose*	kakkiviaq
lips	umilruk
liquor	taanngaq
listen	ata
listen; *is nice to ___ to*	tuharnaarnaqtuq
listens	naalaktuq
lit; *is ___*	ikumajuq
liver	tinguk
lives with him/her	inuuqatigijaa; najuqtaa

living room	ikhivavik
lock	kiluuttaq; kii
locks it	kiiliqtaa; kiluuttaqtaa
long; *is* ___ **(of clothing)**	akuqtujuq
long; *something very* ___	takkarjuaq
long johns	ilulliik
longer; *becomes* ___	takhijuq
longspur; *Lapland* ___	nahaullik
look (command)	takkuuk
look good; *making oneself* ___	ilingaijaqtuq
looks at	tautuktuq
looks attentively	iigijuq; qunngiaqtuq
looks back	qiviaqtuq
looks for ___	qiniqhiajuq; -hiuq
looks for him/her/it	qiniqhiajaa; qiniqtaa
looks in	ittuaqtuq
looks like him/her/it	aadjigijaa; aadjikkutaa
looks up	aarluqtuq
loon; *Arctic* ___	maliriq (*see* qaqhauq, tuullik)
loon; *red-throated* ___	qaqhauq (*see* tuullik, maliriq)
loon; *yellow-billed/king*	tuullik (*see* qaqhauq, maliriq)
loose; *became* ___	ipiiqtuq
loose; *comes* ___	ataiqtuq
loses a game	akimaittuq
loses it	tammaijaa
lost; *is* ___	tammaqtuq
lost weight	qapaktuq
lots; *gets* ___	atqunaqtuq
louse	kumak
louse egg	itqiq
loves him/her/it	piqpagijaa
low; *is* ___	naqittuq
lower part of arm	algaut

lowers him/her/it	anmuktaa
lucky	tuhunnaq
lukewarm; *is* ___	uunnaaqtuq
lung	puvak
lure	qarjuqhaq
lying; *he/she is not* ___	iqunngittuq
lying around	hallaaqtuq

mail carrier	titiqqittijuq
magazine	qun'ngiaq (*see* makpiraaq)
magnet	nipitqaqtaun/nipitqaqtaut/nipitqaqtauti
making a willow mat	uqpiliurniq (*see* avaalaqiaq)
male animal	anguhalluq
male; *human* ___	angun/angut/anguti
man	angut/angun/anguti
man; *married* ___	nulialik
man; *old* ___	inutquaq
manager	aulattiji; ataniq; atanngujaq
mantle for a lamp	ipirakhat; kanguujaq
many	amihut; amigaittut; inugiaktut
many; *how* ___	qaffit
many; *there are* ___	amigaittut; inugiaktut; amihut
March	Qiqailruq
marijuana	higaarluk
marker for making a pattern	titiqtuut/titiqtuun
marker for recognition or identification	naunaitkutaq; naunaipkutaq

marks it for recognition	naunaitkuhiqtaa; naunaipkuhiqtaa
married child and their spouse	qitun'ngat
marrow; *bone* ___	patiq
marrow; *takes the* ___ *out of a bone*	haulluqtuq
marrow; *tool to take the* ___ *out of a bone*	haulluun/haulluut/haulluti
mask	kiinannguaq
mask; *surgical* ___	ivjarun/ivjarut/ivjaruti (*see* ivjaqun)
mat; *door* ___	aluijarvik
mat; *sleeping* ___	avaalaqiaq
mat made of skin (to sit on)	aalliraq
match	ikkin/ikkit/ikkiti (pl. *ikkitit*)
material for making something	hulijakhaq
mates; *a pair of* ___ (animals)	arnautqiik
matter; *it doesn't* ___	takiunniit/takiunniin
matter; *what's the* ___	huva
mattress; *caribou-skin* ___	aalliniq (*see* qaaq, alvakhaq)
May	Qiqaijarluarvia
maybe	ahu; immaqaak
me	uvamnik (*see* uvanga)
measure; *stick to* ___ *the depth of snow*	havgun/havgut/havguti
measures	uuktuqtuq
measures him/her/it	uuktuqtaa
meat	niqi
meat; *boiled* ___	uujuq
meat; *dry* ___	mipku
meat; *frozen* ___ *or fish*	quaq
meat; *raw* ___	mikigaq/mikiraq
mechanic	ingniquhiqiji
meet; *goes to* ___ *him/her/it*	palriaqtaa
meeting place	katimavik; katilvik
meeting; *are having a* ___	katimajut

meets him/her/it	paaqtaa
meets someone by chance	inukhijuq
melted; *has* ___	imaruqtuq; auttuq
melted; *it* ___	mahaktuq
melting; *it is* ___	mahaktiqtuq
melting; *snow is* ___	mahaktuq
melts	auktuqtuq
mends	allaijaijuq
mends a seam	killaijaijuq
mends it (she/he)	allaijaqtaa
mends it (a seam)	killaijaqtaa
menstruates	aunaaqtuq
mentally disabled	ihumakittuq/ihumarluktuq
messy; *has* ___ *hair*	nujarluktuq
middle	qitiq
middle; *the one in the* ___	akulliq
middle-aged person	inirnikhaq
midwife (traditional term)	hanaji
milk	ituk
mind	ihuma
mind; *has already made up his/her/ its* ___	hivunniriiqtuq
minded; *he* ___ *his manners*	ihumaittuq
minister	minihitaq
minutes; *in a few* ___	hadjagu/tadjagu
mirror	tarrijaun/tarrijaut/tarrijauti
miscarriage	ahiruijuq
miss each other by going in different directions or at different times	kaipiktidjutijuk/kaiffiqtidjutijuk/ kaiffiktidjutijuk/kaiffittidjutijuk
misses him/her/it	kinnguqtaa/kinnguijaa
misses the target when shooting	makanngittuq
mistakes him/her/it for someone/ something else	aallaunahugijaa

mitt	pualu/pualuk
mitts; *makes* ___	pualuliuqtuq
mixed milk for baby	amaamakhaliuqtuq
mixes	akujuq
mocks by doing imitations	idjuaqhijuq/igjuaqhijuq
mole	nutibliq/nutipliq
molting bird	ihajuq
Monday	Hananngaut; Hivulli
money	manik
month	tatqiqhiun/tatqiqhiut/tatqiqhiuti
moon	tatqiq
moon is full	tatqiq iluittunnguqtuq
moon; *full* ___	tatqiarikhijuq
moon; *there is a half* ___	tatqiq nappannguqtuq/ navvannguqtuq
moonlit night	tatqiarikhijuq
moose	tuktuvak
more; *some* ___	taitai/haitai (*childish speech*)
more; *wants* ___	pijumaffaaqtuq/pijumphaaqtuq; taitaiffaaqtuq/taitaiphaaqtuq/ haitaiffaaqtuq (*childish speech*)
morning	ublaaq
morning; *this* ___	ublaigami/ublaaq
mosquito	kikturiaq
mosquito net	kikturiilitaq
mosquito's proboscis	qinguq
moss	urjuk
most; *the one who gets the* ___	atqunarnirujuq
mother	amaamak/maamak
mother-in-law (or father-in-law)	haki
motor	ingniqun/ingniqut/ingniquti
motorboat	ingniqutilik
mountain; *side of* ___	majuqqaq
mountain; *small* ___	pinguatigaq

mouth	qaniq
mouth; *closes his/her/its* ___	ipummiqtuq
mouth; *has a sore* ___	qanirluktuq
mouth; *keeps his/her/its* ___ *closed*	ipummingajuq
mouth; *keeps it in his/her/its* ___	uqummiaqtaa
mouth; *opens his/her/its* ___	aittaqtuq
mouth; *roof of* ___	qilaaq
mouthy; *is* ___	qaniqtujuq
moves about	ingutaaqtuq
moves in one spot	aulajuq
moves it to another location	nuutaa
moves to another location	nuuttuq
movie	piksa
movies; *goes to the* ___	piksasuuqtuq (*from English "picture show"*)
mud	marluk
muktuk (skin of whale)	maktak/maktaaq
mumbles	uqamaluktuq
murdered	inuaqtaujuq (*see* tuqutaujuq)
murdered him/her	inuaqtaa (*see* tuqutaa)
murre	atpa
music	atuun/atuut/atuuti
music is playing	atuqtuujaqtuq
musical instrument	atuqtuujaq
muskox	umingmak
muskox; *bull* ___	pangniq
muskox; *young* ___	umingmaaq
muskrat	kivgaluk
mute; *is* ___	uqajuittuq
muzzle; *dog* ___	ivjarun/ivjarut/ivjaruti (*also* ivjaqun)
muzzles it	ivjaruhiqtaa

nail (for building)	kikiak
nail (of finger or toe)	kukik
nail clipper	kukiijaut/kukiijautik
nails it	kikiaktaa
nails it in several places	kikiaktuqtaa
naive; *is* ___	uingajuq
naked; *is* ___	uhiqtuq; uhin'ngajuq; aannuraangiqtuq
name	atiq (pl. atqit)
name; *a* ___ *that must be changed because a child's spirit will not accept it*	atirluktuq
name; *a person with the same name as a close relative*	attiaq (*see* atiq, haunittiaq)
name; *given a* ___ *that mocks him/her*	atiruaqtuq/atirluaqtuq
name; *gives him/her/it a* ___	attiqtaa
name; *same* ___ *but named after different people*	haunittiaq (*see* atiq, attiaq, atiqat, atiqatigiik)
name; *says his/her/its* ___	taijaa
name; *says the* ___ *of a thing or person*	taijuq
name; *two persons having the same* ___	haunittiariik
name; *what's your* ___	kimik atiqaqqit; kinauvit; kina atqin
name; *your* ___	atqin/atqit
names; *says the* ___ *of things*	attiqtuijuq
napkin	ivgun/ivgut/ivguti
narrow	tuattuq
narrow; *there is a* ___ *space in between*	ajanikittuq

navel (umbilicus)	qalahiq
near; *is* ___	qanittuq
nearby	qanilrumi
neck	qunguhiq; qunguhiniq
neck; *nape of the* ___	tunuhiniq
needle; *injection* ___	kapuun/kapuut/kapuuti
needle; *netting* ___ (to repair fishnets)	kuvjin/kuvjit/kuvjiti
needle; *sewing* ___	mitqun/mitqut/mitquti
needle; *threads a* ___	nuvijaa
needles; *gets pins and* ___ *in a limb*	kakilahaijuq
nephew of a male	qangiaq
nephew of a female	nurraq
nephew; *step*___ *of a female*	nurrakhaq
nephew; *step* ___ *of a male*	qangiakhaq
nest	ublu
nest; *flies from its* ___	pikijuq
nest; *makes a* ___	ubluliuqtuq
nest with eggs; *found a* ___	pikiuttuq
nesting bird luring prey away from nest or young	niviuqtuq
nests	ivajuq
net; *catches it with a fish*___	kuvjaqtaa
net; *fish* ___	kuvjaq
net; *sets a fish* ___	kuvjiqtuq; kuvjaqtuqtuq
net; *weight for fish*___	kivvin/kivvit/kivviti; titqaun/titqaut/titqauti
netting needle (to repair fishnets)	kuvjin/kuvjit/kuvjiti
new; *something* ___	nutaaq
newborn (human)	inuhaaq
next; *the* ___ *one*	tugliq
niece of a female	nurraq
niece of a male	ujuruk
niece; *step* ___ *of a female*	nurrakhaq

niece; *step* ___ *of a male*	ujurukhaq
night	unnuaq
night has fallen	unnuktuq
night; *is* ___	unnuliqtuq
night; *last* ___	unnuaq
night; *when* ___ *falls*	unnukpan/unnukpat
nightmare; *has a* ___	itiblijuq
nine	arvinilik pingahut
nipple protector, fur (for breastfeeding dogs, to prevent freezing) (also cap, baby bottle)	muluilitaq
no	imannaq; i'; ih (*slang*)
no; *says* ___	imannaaqtuq; qinngijuq; niaqqulrujuq
nobody; *there is* ___ *there*	inuittuq
noise; *making* ___ *while moving stuff*	pakaktuq
noisy	kukuulaaqtuq(t)/tiitaqtut
none; *there is* ___	piissak
none left; *there is* ___	piittuq
north wind	kanangnaq
northern lights	aqhaliaq; aqhalingiaq
northern lights; *the* ___ *are out*	aqhalialaqijuq; aqhalingialaqijuq
nose (see beak, snout, etc.)	qingaq
nose (not human)	higguk; qingaq
nose; *blows his/her/its* ___	kakkiktuq
nosed; *long-* ___ *or long-beaked animal*	higguqquqtujuq
nothing; *it's* ___	hunngittuq
nothing; *there's* ___ *you can do*	ajurnarman/ajurnarmat
notice; *puts up a* ___	titiqqiqhijuq
November	Hikutirvia
now	tadja/hadja
numb; *is* ___	qaujimaittuq

numerous; *are* ___	amigaittut; inugiaktut; amihut
nurse	munaqhi
nurses its young	ivajuq
nurses; *a baby* ___	amaamaktuq; maamaktuq

oar	paut *(d. pautik)*
oarlock	paurvik; ipulvik
oars; *rows with* ___	pauqtuq
occupied; *is* ___	aliiquhiqtuq
o'clock; *tomorrow at X* ___	aqagu X-munngaqpan/Xmunngaqqan/X-munngaqpat
o'clock; *yesterday at X* ___	ippakhaq x-munngarman/ippakhaq X-munngarmat *(also* ikpakhaq)
October	Tattiarnaqtuq
odour; *an* ___ (see taste)	tipi
odourless (see tasteless)	tipaittuq
off; *gets* ___ *a vehicle or boat*	niujuq
oil delivery person	uqhurjualiqiji
oil; *fuel* ___	uqhurjuaq
oil; *whale* ___	uqhuq
okay; *it's* ___	takiunniit/takiunniin
old man	inutquaq
old woman	aaquaq
old; *how* ___ *are you*	qaffinik ukiuqaqqin/qaffinik ukiuqaqqit
old; *how* ___ *is he/she/it*	qaffinik ukiuqaqqa
old; *something* ___	utuqqaq
older spouse; *married to* ___	angajuaktaq

one	atauhiq
one of a pair	iglua
one; *only* ___	atauhiinnaq
only him/her/it	kihimi; kihiani
open; *is* ___	angmajuq
opening	angmaniq
opens it	angmaqtaa
opponent	akiraq
opponent; *has him/her/it as an* ___	akirarijaa
opponents; *two* ___	akirariik
opposed; *are* ___ *to each other*	hanmitijuk
opposite; *located at the* ___ *end*	akilliq
orange (colour)	aupajangajuq/aupajangattuq
orders him/her/it to do something	pitqujaa
orders someone to do something	pitquijuq
orphan	iliarjuk
other one	aalla
others; *puts it with* ___	ilainnunngaqtaa
otter	pamiuqtuuq
out; *gets* ___ *of a vehicle or boat*	niujuq
out of fire or light; *is* ___	qamittuq
outdoors	hila
outermost	hilalliq
outside	hilami
outside; *goes* ___	anijuq
outside; *is* ___	hilamiittuq
outside; *on the* ___ *of him/her/it*	hilataani
outside; *puts him/her/it* ___	anitaa
over here; *place it* ___	hamunga
over there	taavani

overloaded; *is* ____	uhiliqpallaaqtuq
overtakes him/her/it	qaangiqtaa (*see* apquhaaqtaa)
owl; *snowy* ____	ukpik

packsack	nangmaktaq
packs a baby on his/her back	amaaqtuq
packs something on the back	nangmaktuq
paddle	paut (d. *pautik*)
paddles	pauqtuq
page	makpiraq
page; *turns the* ____	makpiraqtuq
pail	qattaq
pain; *feels a* ____	uluriahuktuq
painful; *is* ____	ulurianaqtuq
paint	minguk
paints	minguliqhijuq
paints it	minguktaa
pair	iglugiik
pair; *is missing one of a* ____	igluittuq
pair; *mating* ____ *of animals*	arnautqiik
pair; *one of a* ____	iglu
pair; *uses both of a* ____	igluktuqtuq
pair; *uses only one of a* ____	iglupiaqtuqtuq
palate	qilaaq
palm of hand	itimak
pants	qarliik
pants are falling down	hituliqtuq

pants have fallen down	hitujuq
paper	alilajuq; titiraakhaq; titiraakhaut/ titiraakhaun; titiraq
paper to hide trap when trapping	qilaaq
parent	angajuqqaaq
parents of your child's spouse	qitun'ngaqat/qitun'ngaqatit
parka	atigi
parka; *bottom of hood on a packing* ___	puvviujaq
parka; *outside caribou-skin* ___	qulittaq
parka; *white* ___ *for hunting*	qatirnitaq
parka; *woman's* ___ *for packing a baby on her back*	amaun/amaut/amauti
part	ila
partner in doing or making something	piqati
pass; *makes room for him/her/it to* ___	apqutiniktaa
passed by (travelling on ice or water)	kitauttuq
passes at a distance	kitautiqtuq
passes away	huiqtuq
passes him/her/it	qaangiqtaa (*see* apquhaaqtaa)
pastime	tuninnguitkutikhaq
patch; *to* ___ *before it wears out or opens*	qaammiruhuktuijuq
patches it	ilaaqtuqtaa/ilaaqtaa
path	apquhiniq
patient; *is* ___	palviittuq
patient; *is always* ___	mamiahujuittuq
paw; *dog's* ___	alurnaq
payment; *something used as* ___	akilijjun/akilijjut/akilijjuti
pays for it	akiliqtaa
peculiar; *looks* ___	takummarluktuq
pee; *has to go* ___	quuhuktuq

INUINNAQTUN TO ENGLISH

peels a fruit, vegetable	amiraijaijuq
peels it	amiraijaqtaa
peels off	qaatiqtuq
peg; *clothes____*	tingittaitkut/tingittaitkun/ tingittaipkut/tingittaipkun
pen	titiraun/titiraut/titrauti
penis	uhuk
perfume	tipigikhaut
person	inuk
person of mixed blood, part white	Qablunaavjak
person; *a white ____*	Qablunaaq
person; *an Inuk____*	Inuinnaq
person; *a First Nations ____*	Itqiliq
person; *is a ____*	inuujuq
Peterhead	Umiujaq
pets it	pattaaqtaa
phalarope; *red ____ (drifter)*	haavraq
pick them (up)	pukukkit
pickaxe	nunaliqun; nunaliqut
picks berries	pukuktuq
picks on someone	nanngudjijuq; nannguttijuq
picture; *takes his/her/its ____*	piksaliuqtaa
piece	ila
piece of a broken object	ahiqquq; navvaq
piece; *a usable ____ or part*	ilakhaq
pillow	akin/akit/akiti
pilot	aquti
pimple	pukkuq
pinches	puudjuktuq
pink	aupajaavjaktuq
pins and needles	kakilahaaq
pins; *gets ____ and needles in a limb*	kakilahaijuq
pinworm	qauqtaq

pipe	tuqhuaq; paipak
pipe tobacco	paipaut
pit or stone of a fruit	hauniq
pities him/her/it	nagligijaa
pitiful; *is* ___	naglingnaqtuq
pitiful; ___ *looking*	ilingaittuq
place	ini
place; *takes his/her/its* ___	himmauhiqtaa
place; *there is no* ___	inikhaittuq
places it	ilijaa
plain; *a* ___ (flat land)	natirnaq
plane	tingmit
plane (tool)	hanirarmik
plane (traditional tool)	havruut
plane; *uses a wood* ___	hanirarmiktuq
plans; *makes* ___	hivunikhaqhiuqtuq
plant	nauttiaq
plate	akkiutaq
platform; *snow* ___ *around outside of iglu*	qaamiutaq
play; *are* ___*ing skin toss, blanket toss*	avataaqtaqtut
plays	piujaqtuq; ulapqijuq
plays fiddle	uluaraqtuq; agiraqtuq
plays with a toy	ulapqiujaqtuq
pleased; *is* ___	qujajuq
pliers	kingmautik; tiggutik
plover; *golden* ___	tuulligiaq
plucks a bird	iritaqtuq
plumber	tuqhualiqiji
pocket	kauttuaq
pocket; *keeps it in his/her* ___	kauttuarmiutarijaa
pocket; *puts it in his/her own* ___	kauttuarminunngaqtaa
point	nuvuk

point of land	hingik
polar bear	nanuq
polar bear; *gets a* ___	nanuqtuq
polar bear; *young* ___	nanuaq
pond	tahiraq
poor; *does* ___ *work*	pidjarluktuq; pimmarluktuq
poor; *is* ___	ilingajuq
porch	tuqhuuk
portage	itivjaaq
portage; *short* ___	atanikittuq
pot or pan with a handle	ipualik; hiqanaaqhiun
pot; *cooking* ___	utkuhik
pot; *huge* ___	qattarjuaq; qattarjuk
pouch; *tobacco* ___	tipaakuun
prayer	qin'ngaun
praying	qin'ngaqtuq
prays	qin'ngaqtuq/qin'raqtuq
pregnant; *is* ___	hingaijuq
presence; *in his* ___	takkuani
presence; *in my* ___	takkumni
presence; *in your* ___	takkurni
present; *a* ___ *given*	aittuun/aittuut/aittuuti
pressure ridge	quglungniq
pretty	pinniqhaqtaa
price	aki
probably	ahu; immaqaak
propeller	anguun/anguut/anguuti
propels	anguaqtuq
protective sheath, made of fur, for male dog's penis (to prevent freezing)	uhuilitaq
ptarmigan; *rock* ___	aqilgiq
ptarmigan; *willow* ___	aqilgivik
puddles from something dripping	kuhirnirit

puffed up; *is* ___	publaumajuq
puffs up	publaktuq
pulls (of a dog)	qimuktuq
pulls him/her/it	uniaqtaa; nuqitaa; qimuktaa
pump; *air* ___	publiut/publiun
punches dough	akuttijuq
pupil of the eye	ijaruvak
puppy	qinmiarjuk
purple	tungujuktuq
pushes him/her/it	pingujaa
pushes it back	tatijaa
puts his/her own clothes on	aannuraaqtuq
puts it down	ilijaa
putting shoes/boots on the wrong feet	haqpingajuq

quarrelsome; *is* ___	qaniqtujuq
question	apiqhuun/apiqhuut/apiqhuuti
question; *asks a* ___	apiqhijuq
questions	apiqhuqtuq
quits	taimaaqtuq

races	aqpaluarutijuk; tikiqqaaqhautijut; uliisiqtuq
racing	tikitqaaqhautijut
radio	naalaun/naalaut/naalauti
rag for wiping	ivgun/ivgut/ivguti
rain	nipaluk
rainbow	ajagutaq/ajakutaq
rains	nipalliqtuq
rake	haqiktaun/haqiktaut/haqiktauti
rat	ulimakkak
raven	tulugaq
razor	umngijauti
reach; *cannot ___ a place*	ajuqhittuq
reaches it	tikitaa
reads	taiguaqtuq
reads it	taiguaqtaa
ready	taki
ready; *gets ___*	itqanaijaqtuq; parnaijaqtuq; upalungaijaqtuq; hannaijaqtuq
ready; *is ___*	hannaiqtuq; iqqanaiqtuq; itqanaiqtuq
rear	kingulliq
rear; *in the ___ part of ...*	kinguani
rear; *in the ___ part of a boat*	aquani
received; *a gift ___*	aittuuhiaq
receives a gift	aittuuhiaqtuq
receives it as a payment	akiliuhiarijaa
recites the names of things	attiqtuijuq
recognizable; *is ___*	ilitarnaqtuq
recognizes him/her/it	ilitarijaa

record album	atuqtuujaq
recorder; *tape* ___	nipiliun/nipiliut/nipiliuti; nipiliurun/nipiliurut/nipiliuruti
recording tape	nipikhaun/nipikhaut/nipikhauti
records; *tape* ___	nipiliuqtuq
recovers from an illness	akuliarikhijuq
red	aupajaaqtuq
red fox	kajuqtuq
redpoll	hakhagiaq
reef	ikkalruq/itkalruq
refills it	immitqiktaa
refused; *is* ___ *something*	annirutijaujuq
refuses	pijumanngittuq
refuses him/her/it	annirutijaa
regretful; *is* ___	hain'ngihuktuq/hain'ngiguhuktuq/hainrihuktuq/hainriguhuktuq
related persons (two)	ilagiik
relative	ila; ilaruhiq; qitun'ngaq
relative; *is his/her/its* ___	ilaruhirijaa; ilagijaa
remember; *tries to* ___	itqakhaijuq/itqaqhaqtuq
remembers	itqaqtuq
remembers him/her/it	itqaqtaa
remnants	amiakkut
removes a baby from an amaut	niujuq
repairs	hanajuq
repairs it	hanajaa
repairs; *needs frequent* ___	havagluqutainnannguqtuq
replaces him/her/it	himmauhiqtaa
researcher	ihivriuqhiji
researches it	ihivriuqtaa
resembles him/her/it	aadjigijaa; aajjikkutaa
respect	ihumagijauttiarniq
restless legs; *has* ___	patirialaqijuq

rests	unaguiqhiqtuq
retaliation; *receiving ___ after being mean or irritating for a long time*	manittuq
returns	utiqtuq
revenge; *takes ___*	akiraqtuqtuq
revenge; *takes ___ on him/her/it*	akiraqtuqtaa
rheumatism; *has ___*	nukigliurniq
rib	tulimaaq
rice	haviqquujaq
ridgepole	nalariaq
rifle	hiqquqtiun/hiqquqtiut/hiqquqtiuti; hiqquqtijjun/hiqquqtijjut/ hiqquqtijjuti
right?	ai?
right side	taliqpik
right; *fits just ___*	nalaumajuq
right; *is ___*	ihuaqtuq
right; *on his/her/its ___*	taliqpiani
right; *on my ___*	taliqpimni
right; *on your ___*	taliqpingni
right-handed	taliqpingmuuqtuq
rime	patuk; ilu
ring	mikilirarmiaq
ringing; *it keeps on ___ (one long ring)*	hivajaaqtuq
rings	hivajaqtaaqtuq
rings once	hivajaqtuq
ripples; *makes ___*	qalairaqtuq
rises	publaktuq
rises; *dough ___*	publakhiijuq
river	kuugaq
road	apqun/apqut/apquti
road; *makes a ___*	apquhiuqtuq

road; *there is no* ___	apqutaittuq
roadway; *there is no more* ___	apqutaiqtuq
roasts something	algiqhiijuq
rock	ujarak
rock cairn (inukshuk)	inukhuk
rocky area	ujaraktujuq
rod; *jiggling* ___ **(for jigging fish)**	aulajjun
roe	huvak
rolls	akhaktuq
roof	qilaanga
room	igluaq
room; *bed*___	hinigvik
room; *makes* ___ *for him/her/it*	ininiktaa
room; *makes* ___ *for him/her/it to pass* **(on a road)**	apqutiniktaa
room; *makes* ___ *for someone/ something*	ininikhijuq
room; *there is* ___	inikhaqaqtuq
room; *there is a lot of* ___	initujuq; inikhaqquqtujuq
room; *there is little* ___	inikhaqqukittuq
room; *there is no* ___	inikhaittuq
root; *edible* ___	mahuk/mahu
rope	akhunaaq
rope or chain to tie dogs or boats	ipiutaq
rope; *bearded seal skin used to make* ___	alikhaq
rotten; *is* ___	aujuq
rows	pauqtuq
rudder	aquun/aquut/aquuti
ruler	uuktuun/uuktuut/uuktuuti; uuktaun/ uuktaut/uuktauti
rumen	tunuhitaq
running; *starts* ___	aqpahijuq
runs	aqpattuq

runs away	aqpajuaqtuq
runs on all fours	pangaliktuq
rushes	irinahuktuq
rust	qattiniq
rusted; *is* ___	qattinnaktuq
rutting male seal	tiggak
rutting seal; *smell of* ___	tiggakhungni

S

sad; *is* ___	akhaarniq
safe; *is* ___	annaktuq
sail	titqalaarut/titqalaut/titqautaq
sailing	titqalaaqtuq
salt; *puts* ___ *on it*	tarjuliqtuqtaa/tariuliqtuqtaa
salty	tariurnittuq; hiipangnittuq
same; *they (two) are the* ___	aadjikkutaa, aadjigiiiktuk
same; *they (two) are the* ___ *size*	aktikkutariik
sand	hiuraq
sandbar (or shallows)	ikkalruq/itkalruq
sandpiper; *white-rumped* ___	higjariaq
satiated; *is* ___	aqiattuqtuq
Saturday	Saaluti/Havangnairvik
saucer	aalliraujaq
saw	uluaqtuun
saws it	uluaqtaa
saws it up	uluaqtuqtaa
says his/her/its name	taijaa
says no by shaking his/her/its head	niaqqulrujuq

says something	nipliqtuq/nibliqtuq
says the names of things	attiqtuijuq
scale; *fish* ___	kapihik
scared; *is* ___	iqhijuq; kappiahuktuq
scared; *is* ___ *of him/her/it*	iqhigijaa; kappiagijaa
scarf around face	ivjarun/ivjarut/ivjaruti (*also* ivjaqun)
scarf; *puts a* ___ *around someone's face*	ivjaruhiqtaa
scary; *is* ___	iqhinaqtuq; kappianaqtuq
scent; *has a nice* ___	tivjariktuq
school	iliharvik; sikuurvik
scissors	kivjautik
scissors; *cuts it with* ___	kivjaqtaa
scoop; *ice* ___	ilaun/ilaut/ilauti
scoops the ice from a fishing hole	ilauqtuq
scratches an itch	kumiktuq
scree	akhaarniq
screen (for seal hunting)	taluquaq; talu
sculpin	kanajuq
sculpin; *small* ___	kanajuraq
sea urchin	itqujaq
sea; *goes towards the* ___	tarjuliaqtuq; tariuliaqtuq
sea; *travels by* ___	tarjukkuuqtuq/tariukkuuqtuq
seal	nattiq
seal breathing hole; *looking for a* ___ *under the snow*	mauliqtuq (*see* nippaqtuq, atiqtuq)
seal breathing holes; *asking to look for* ___ *under the snow before seal hunting*	mauligaqujaanga
seal is lying on the ice surface	qakipqajuq
seal makes a breathing hole	agluliuqtuq
seal pup	nattiaq
seal that crawls far from its breathing hole	paannguliaq/paamnguliaq/paanruliaq

seal's breathing hole	aglu
seal; *bearded* ___	ugjuk
seal; *female* ___	nuniq
seal; *gets a* ___	nattiqtuq
seal; *ringed* ___	nattiq
seal; *rutting male* ___	tiggak
seal; *rutting male* ___ *stinks*	ajulaqtuq (*see* tiggak)
seal; *small* ___	utajuraq; nattiaq
seal; *waits at a* ___'s *breathing hole*	nippaqtuq/nikpaqtuq
seal; *young bearded* ___	ugjugaq/ugjuaq
seal; *young bearded* ___ *with white fur*	pualulik
seam; *mends a* ___	killaijaijuq
search; *in* ___ *of something*	nalvaaqhiuqtuq
searches	qiniqhiajuq; -hiuq
searches for him/her/it	qiniqtaa
searching with the flashlight lit	naniruaqtuq
seashell	uviluq
seated; *is* ___	ikhivajuq
seaweed	aqajat
second; *the* ___ *one*	tugliq
secretary	titiraqti
see you again sometime	ilaanilu; ilaanittauq; qakuguttauq
see you later today	ublumittauq
see; *cannot* ___ *well*	takpiittuq
sees	takujuq
sees him/her/it	takujaa
sees him/her/it clearly	takummarikhijaa
sees well	takpiktuq
seized; *is* ___	aqhaaqtaujuq
seizes him/her/it	aqhaaqtaa
September	Apitilirvik
servant/maid	kivgaq

servant/maid; *works as a* ___	kivgaqtuqtuq
sets (as the sun)	pulaliqtuq
seven	arvinilik atauhiq
sewage truck	anaqtaun/anaqtaut/anaqtauti
sewage truck driver	anaqtautiliqiji
sewing machine	miqhuqtitaq
sewing needle	mitqun/mitqut/mitquti
sews	miqhuqtuq
sews it	miqhuqtaa
sex; *has* ___	kujaktuq
sex; *has* ___ *with a man*	angutituqtuq
shadow	tarraq
shaggy; *has* ___ *hair*	tulrujuq
shakes	uulijuq
shakes hands with...	aatituuqtuq
shallow; *is* ___	ikkattuq/itkattuq
shaman	angatkuq
share equally	avguumattiarniq
sharp edge of knife or axe	ipikharniq
sharp tool	hatku
sharp; *is* ___	ipiktuq
sharp; *it is no longer* ___	ipiiqtuq
sharpener	ipikhaun
sharpens it	ipikhaqtaa
sharpens something	ipikhaijuq
shattered	hiqummiktuq
shaves	umngijaqtuq
shed; *has* ___ *all its hair, fur, or feathers*	mitquiqtuq
shed; *has* ___ *half its fur*	qalingujuq
shedding its fur	irijuq (*see* qalingujuq)
sheep	imnaiq
shelf	iliqpik; iliuqpik

shiny; *is becoming* ___	qiblarikhijuq; qiblaqhiqtuq
ship	umiaqpak
shivers	uulijuq
shoelace	hingiq
shooting; *is good at* ___	makaqhuqtuq
shooting; *is good at* ___ *with a bow and arrow*	pitikhuqtuq
shooting; *misses the target when* ___	makanngittuq
shoots at him/her/it	hiquriaqtaa
shoots at someone/something	hiquriaqtuq
shoots it/him/her	makaqtaa
shoots too high	qalruttaa
shoots too low	tungauttuq
shoots to the side	igluaqtuq
shoots with a gun	hiquqtuq
shoots with an arrow	pitikhaqtuq
shop; *a* ___	niuvvaavik
shore	hinaa
shore; *boat reaches the* ___	tulaktuq; apuqtuq
shore; *goes along the* ___ *of a lake, sea, or river*	hinaaguuqtuq
shore; *ocean* ___	higjaq
shore; *on the opposite* ___	akiani
short; *is* ___	naittuq
short; *is* ___ *(of clothing)*	akukittuq
shortest; *by the* ___ *way*	qanilrukkut/qanilrukkun
shot; ___ *it on the side*	igluaqtaa
shoulder	tui *(d. tuik)*
shoulder blade	kiahik *(d. kiattik)*
shoulders; *carries something on his/her/its* ___	kakaktuq
shovel	pualrin/pualrit/pualriti *(d. pualritiik; pl. pualrittit)*

shovels	pualrihaqtuq
shovels it	pualrihaqtaa
show; *goes to the* ___	piksasuuqtuq (*from "picture show"*)
shows it	hatqummiqtaa
shows up	nuitajuq; hatqummiqtuq; hatqiqtuq
shrinks	mikhijuq
shy; *is* ___	kan'nguhuktuq
siblings	nukariit; angajugiit
sick; *is* ___	aanniaqtuq
side	haniraq; hani
sideways	hanningajuq
sighing	aniqhaumijaaqtuq
sighs	aniqhaummiktuq
sight; *looks through* ___	qinngunmiktuq
sight; *telescopic* ___	qinngun
sinew (before it becomes ivalu)	uliut/uliun
sinew (for sewing)	ivalu
sings	huqullaaqtuq; atuqtuq; ingiuqtuq
sings a drum dance song	ingiuqtuq
sink	uaqhivik
sinks	kivijuq
sip; *takes a* ___	hiluraqtuq
sips	niuqhijuq; imiqtuq; -tuq-; niuqqaqtuq
sister; *older* ___ *of a female* (older sibling, same sex)	angajuk
sister; *older* ___ *of a male*	aliqak
sister; *older step*___ *of a female*	angajukhaq
sister; *older step*___ *of a male*	aliqakhaq
sister; *younger* ___ *of a female*	nukaq
sister; *younger* ___ *of a male*	najak
sister; *younger step*___ *of a female*	nukakhaq
sister; *younger step*___ *of a male*	najakhaq
sister-in-law (wife of husband's younger brother)	nukaunnguq (*compare* angajunnguq)

INUINNAQTUN TO ENGLISH

sister-in-law of a male	ainnuaq; aik
sister-in-law of female (wife of husband's older brother)	angajunnguq (*compare* nukaunnguq or ukuaq)
sits down	ingittuq
six	arvinilik
size; *they (two) are the same* ___	aktikkutariik
skates	sikiiraqtuq
skating	quahijaaqtuq (*see* sikiiraqtuq)
skies	hilarjuaq; qilak
skin of a fish	amiraq
skin of fruit	amiraq
skin; *animal* ___	amiq (d. *ammak*, pl. *amrit*)
skin; *are playing* ___ *toss, blanket toss*	avataaqtaqtut
skin; *human* ___	uvinik
skin; *seal* ___	amiq (d. *ammak*, pl. *amrit*)
skinned; *is* ___	amiiqtuq
skinning knife	aaktuut; aagut
skins it	amiiqtaa
skins something	aaktuqtuq; amiijaijuq
skipping	avataaqtaqtut
skirt	akurun/akurut/akuruti
skua; *Arctic* ___ *(see jaeger)*	ihunngaq
sky	qilak
sky is clearing up	allaliqtuq
slaps him/her/it	patiktaa
sled	aalliak
sled runner	pilraaq (d. *pilraak*)
sled; *crosspiece on a* ___	napu
sled; *curved tip of* ___ *runner*	uirniq
sled; *hole to pass the rope through on a* ___	pukkuk
sled; *rope for tying crosspieces of a* ___	napuliut

sled; *travels by* ___	aalliaqtuqtuq
sleep; *didn't* ___ *well*	hinnarluktuq
sleep; *trying to go to* ___	hinnakhaqtuq
sleeps	hiniktuq
sleeps for a long time	hinikhaaqtuq
sleeps soundly	hinnariktuq
sleeve	aiq (d. *attik*, pl. *attit*)
slices it	avguqtaa
slices up	avguijuq
slides (once)	hituaqtuq; anmuujuq
sliding (playing)	hituaqattaqtuq
slimmed; *has* ___ *down*	qapaktuq
sling (for arm)	ikuhiun/ikuhiut/ikuhiuti
slingshot	illuut/illuutik
slipper; *inner* ___	ilipiruq
sloppy; *is* ___	pimmarluktuq; pidjarluktuq
slow; *is* ___	kajumiittuq
small; *is* ___	mikijuq; -nnuaq; -arjuk
smaller one	mikitqijaq
smaller; *gets* ___	mikhijuq
smart; *very* ___	ihumatujuq
smell; *a* ___	tipi
smell; *has no* ___ (scent)	tipaittuq
smells bad	naqujaqtuq/tipjarluktuq
smells bad (of pipe tobacco)	tivjarluktuq
smells good (of food)	mamaqhungnittuq
smells something	naimajuq
smelt	kakilahak
smiles	qungujuktuq
smoke	pujuq; ihiq
smokes a cigarette	higaaqtuq
smokes marijuana	higaarluktuq
smothers	ipijuq

INUINNAQTUN TO ENGLISH

snare	nigaq
snare; *catches it in a* ___	nigaqtaa
snares something	nigaqtuq
snares; *uses* ___	nigaqtuqtuq
snatched; *is* ___	aqhaaqtaujuq
sneezes	tagiuqtuq/tagjuqtuq
sniffles	kakkiliqtaqtuq; niurmiktuq
sniffs	niurmiktuq; kakkiliqtaqtuq
snores	qamnguqtuq
snores; *habitually* ___	qamnguinnaqtuq
snout	higguk; qingaq
snow blowing along a surface	natiruvilaqijuq
snow bunting (snowbird)	amaulikkaaq
snow goose	kanguq
snow melts	mahaktuq
snow or dust is blowing behind a moving vehicle	natiruvilaqutijuq
snow to make water	aniu
snow; *fallen* ___	apun/aput/aputi
snow; *falling* ___	qanniq
snow; *falling powder* ___	minguliq
snow; *fetches* ___ *to make water*	aniutaqtuq
snow; *fine sugar* ___	pukaq
snow; *first* ___ *in autumn*	apiqun/apiqut/apiquti
snow; *fresh soft* ___	aqilluqqaq
snow; *frosty, sparkling* ___	patuqun
snow; *is blowing powder* ___	mingulilaqijuq
snow; *is buried in* ___	apittuq
snow; *is covered with* ___	apijuq
snow; *is covered with frosty, sparkling* ___	patuqutaujuq
snow; *is in the* ___	apihimajuq
snow; *light soft* ___	qaniaq
snow; *melting* ___	mahak

snow; *melts ice or ___ to make water*	immiuqtuq
snow; *new fallen ___*	qanniqut
snow; *powder ___*	minguliq
snow; *powder ___ is falling*	minguliruqtuq
snow; *sugar ___*	pukak
snow; *takes the ___ off*	aputaijaijuq
snow; *takes the ___ off him/her/it*	aputaijaqtaa
snowbank	aputtaaq/ukharjuk
snow-blind; *is ___*	illuktuq
snowblock	auviq; qarmakhaq
snowblock that goes into top hole of an iglu	qilaqqaun
snowblocks; *cuts ___*	auviuqtuq; qarmakhaliuqtuq
snowblocks; *right place to cut ___*	auvvivik; qarmakhaqtarvik
snowdrift carved by the wind	qimugjuk
snowflake	qanik
snowhouse	iglu
snowing; *it is ___ wet snow*	minguliqtuq
snowmobile	sikiituuk (*from "skidoo"*)
snowmobiling; *goes ___*	sikiituuqtuq
snows softly	qaniaqtuq
snows; *it ___*	qanniqtuq
so	hunauvva
soaked with liquid	mihuktuq
soap	irmiun/irmiut/irmiuti
soapstone (for making cooking pots)	utkuhikhaq/ukkuhikhaq
soapstone; *has lots of ___*	ulukhaqtuuq
soccer; *playing ___*	itingmigaqtuq
sock; *caribou-skin ___*	aliqti (d. *aliqtik*)
sock; *short duffle ___*	piniraq (d. *piniqqak*)
soft drink	kukukuulaq
soft; *is ___*	aqittuq

soft; *is ___ and warm*	nirumiktuq
soldering iron	auktirun/auktirut/auktiruti
soldier	angujakti
sole of boot/foot	alluk *(d. allak)*
sole; *boot ___ made from sealskin*	atungaq (d. *atungak*)
sole; *moosehide ___*	tuktuvalik (d. *tuktuvallak*)
some time ago	imani
something; *is looking for ___ to do*	hulijakhaqhiuqtuq
something that you are pulling (tied up) that comes to a sudden halt	qillukkittuq
sometime; *see you ___*	qakuguttauq
sometime; *see you again ___*	ilaanilu; ilaanittauq
sometimes	ilaani
somewhere else	aallami; ahini
son	irniq
son; *only ___*	irnituaq
son; *step___*	irnikhaq
son-in-law	ningauk
song	atuut/atuun/atuuti
song; *drum dance ___*	pihiq
soon (in a few minutes)	hadjagu/tadjagu
soot	pauq
soot; *full of ___*	pauttuq
sore; *a ___*	kilaaq
sore/infected throat; *has a ___*	iggiarliqtuq/iggiarliuqtuq
sorry	mamianaq
soul	anirniq
sound	nipi
sound; *makes a continuous ___*	nivjaaqtuq
south wind	pingangnaq
spacious	nirutujuq
spade	nunaliqun; nunaliqut
spade (in a deck of cards)	kapuun

speak; *cannot* ___	uqajuittuq
speaks	uqaqtuq
speaks better	uqqarikhijuq
speaks to him/her/it	uqautijaa
speaks well	uqqariktuq
speaks with a low voice	ihivjuktuq
spear	kapuun/kapuut/kapuuti
spear; *three-pronged fishing* ___	kakivak; nuijaaqpak
Spence Bay (former name)	Talurjuaq/Taloyoak
spends the summer	aujijuq
spider	aahivak
spills	kuvijuq/kuvihijuq
spills it	kuvijaa
spinal column	kuapikkat *(sing. kuapigaq)*; qimirluk
spinal cord	qitiraq
spine	qimirluk; kuapikkat *(sing. kuapigaq)*
spinning top	kaiptaq
spins around	kaivaluaqtuq
spins it around something	kaivjaqtaa; qipitiqtaa/qiputiqtaa
spinster	uilgahuk
spits blood	adjiqijuq
spits it out	uriaqtuq/uriuqtuq
spits up	hittuqittuq
splash; *makes a* ___	hiqiqtuq
splashes	hiqqaqtuq
splashes repeatedly	hiqiraqtuq
spokesperson	uqaqti
spoon	aluun/aluut/aluuti
spot; *dark* ___ *in the distance*	madjaaqtuq
spouse	inuuqati; aippaq
spread; *has his/her legs* ___	ablaangajuq
spring	upin'ngaaq/upinraaq
spring; *coiled* ___	ihivjuraq

spring; *early* ___	upin'ngakhaq/upinrakhaq
spruce tree	qijuvik/qiuvik
square	kikkariktuq
squeak; *makes a ___ing sound when walking on snow/gravel*	qikaaqtuq
squints	qinngurluktuq
stabs him/her/it	kapijaa
stabs himself/herself/itself	kapijuq
stabs someone/something	kapihijuq
staggers	ulruaqhijuq
stain	halumailruq
stain; *a ___ where something has dripped*	kuhirniq
stairs	tunmirautit
stalks an animal	tarraqtuqtuq
stand; *removable* ___	ajakutaaq/ajagutaaq
stands it up	makitaa
stands on it	nangirvigijaa
stands up	nangiqtuq
stands up (from prone or sitting position)	makittuq
stands upright	napajuq
star	ubluriaq
stares	iigijuq; qun'ngiaqtuq
stares at him/her/it	iigijaa
starfish	algaujaq
startle; *is easy to* ___	qugluktaaqtuq
startled; *is* ___	qugluktuq
startles him/her/it	qugluktitaa
starts a skidoo, truck, etc.	ikitaqtuq
starves (to death)	aqiaruaqtuq
stays out in camp	aullaqhimajuq
stays up late	pigaaqtuq
stays with him/her/it	najuqtaa

steals	kukiktuq; tigliktuq
steals it	tigliktaa; kukiktaa
steam	ihiq
step; *takes a* ___	abluqtuq
stepbrother of a female	anikhaq
stepfather	angutikhaq; aappakhaq
stepmother	maamakhaq; amaamakhaq; arnakhaq
stepniece of a male	ujurukhaq
steps down from	atqaujuq
steps; *takes large* ___	aptuniqtujuq
steps; *takes small* ___	aptunikittuq
stepstool	tungmiqqat
stern of a boat; *rear part of a boat*	aqu
stern; *goes to the* ___	aqumuktuq
stern; *in the* ___ *of a boat*	aquani
stick; *is easy to* ___	nipittaaqtuq
sticks to something	nipinngajuq; nipittuq
stick; ___ *used to trim qulliq wick*	atqun/atqut/atquti
sticky; *is* ___	nipitqaqtuq
still (duration)	huli
still (not moving)	nutqangajuq
stingy; *is* ___	anniruhuktuq
stinks	tipaaqtuq
stirs	akujuq
stocking (borrowed from English)	hitaakiq *(d. hitaakik)*
stomach	aqiaruq *(see* nadjak*)*
stomach; *first* ___ *of caribou*	tunuhitaq
stomach ache; *has a* ___	aqiarurliqtuq; aqiarurliuqtuq; naarliuqtuq; nadjagliqtuq
stone	ujarak
stone; *fall of* ___	akhaarniq
stones	ujaraliaq
stop!	taimak

stops	taimaaqtuq
stops for awhile	nutqangajuq
stops moving	nutqaqtuq
storage place	iliuqpik; iliqpik
store	niuvirvik; situa
storm	hilarluk/hilaluk; piqtuq
stormy; *is* ___	hilarluktuq/hilaluktuq; piqtuq
story	unipkaaq
story; *tells a* ___ *or legend*	unipkaaqtuq
stove	ingnirvik
stove; *Primus* ___	hiurjuk
straight; *goes in a* ___ *line*	narlungajuq
stranger	tuurmiaq
strap around the chest for securing a backpack	nangmautaq
stretch; *can* ___	tahittaaqtuq
stretched out	tahittuq
stretcher (for carrying injured person)	akirautik
stretches it out	tahitaa
stretches something	tahitirijuq
string	qivjaq
string game	ajaraaq
string games; *plays* ___	ajaraaqtuq
string used for string games	ajaraun/ajaraut/ajarauti
strokes him/her/it	pattaaqtaa
strong; *is* ___	hakugiktuq
stroud	hukkinaaq
stuck; *is* ___	ajuqhittuq
sucks	milukaqtuq
sucks; *a baby* ___ *milk*	maamaktuq; amaamaktuq
sufficient; *is* ___	naammaktuq
suffocates	ipijuq
sugar	aukhiriaq

summer	aujaq
summer; *goes to spend the* ___	aujijaqtuqtuq
sun	hiqiniq
sun; *is shining brightly*	hiqinnaaqtuq
sunburst; *making a* ___ (style of parka hood trim, made of wolf, from the Western Arctic)	puhittijuq
Sunday	Unaguiqhirvik; Hanahuilrun/Hanahuilrut
sunset	hiqiniq pulaliqtuq
supper; *eats* ___	nullauhiqtuq
surely	aniqtak
surprised; *he* ___ *him/her/it*	upin'ngaqtaa
surprised; *is* ___	upinngaqhiqtuq
surrounding area	qanilruq; avalu
surrounding; *in the* ___ *area*	qanilrumi
suspenders	nuqhutik
swallows it	iijaa
swallows something	iihijuq
swallows the wrong way	hittuqittuq
swan; *whistling* ___	qugjuk
sweats (animal or person)	nunijuq
sweeps/rakes	haqiktaqtuq
sweet; *is* ___	hiirnaqtuq
swell; *ocean* ___	tagjaaq
swells up	puvittuq
swells; *there are* ___	tagjaaqtuq
swims	naluujaqtuq
swimsuit	naluujauti
switch; *electrical* ___	ikittaun

table	ikpan/ikpat/ikpati
table; *coffee* ___	ikpataujaq
table; *small* ___	ikpataujaq
tablespoon	aluutirjuaq
tail of a bird	papik
tail of fish	papiruq
tail of land mammals	pamiuq
tail of a whale	haqpik
tail; *moves its* ___ (of fish and sea mammals)	papiqqiqijuq
tail; *wags its* ___	pamirraaqtuq
tailbone	pamialluk
take off; *ready to* ___	tingmikhajuq
takes it away from him/her/it	aqhaaqtaa
takes it off	piiqtaa
talks	uqaqtuq
talks about him/her/it	uqauhirijaa
talks to him/her/it	uqarvigijaa
talks with him/her/it	uqaqatigijaa
tall	angijuq; -qpak; -rjuaq
tall; *is as* ___ *as*	angitigijuq
tangled; *are* ___	illaktut; ilaktut
tape for recording	nipikhaun/nipikhaut/nipikhauti
tape recorder	nipiliurun/nipiliurut/nipiliuruti; nipiliun/nipiliut/nipiliuti
tapeworm	qumaq
taps	apkaluktaqtuq
tarpaulin	higjaaq
taste; *a* ___	tipi

taste; *has a bad* ___	naqujaqtuq
taste; *likes the* ___ *or smell of it*	mamarijaa
tastes bad (of bad tobacco)	tivjarluktuq
tastes good	tivjariktuq/mamaqtuq
tasty	tivjariktuq
tattles	unnirluktuq
tattoo; *facial* ___	kakiniq
tea	tii
tea; *drinks* ___	tiituqtuq
tea; *leaf* ___	tiirluk
tea; *makes* ___	tiiliuqtuq
tea; *place to make* ___	tiiliurvik/tiiliurun
tea bag; *used* ___	tiirluk
tea set; *playing with a* ___	qallutaujaqtuq
teacher	ilihaiji
teaches	ilihaijuq
teaches him/her/it	ilihautijaa (*see* ilihaijaa)
teaches it	ilihaijaa (*see* ilihautijaa)
teapot	tiiliurun; tiiliurvik
tear (as in crying)	qulvik
tear; *can* ___	alilaaqtuq
tearing	qulvijuq
tears	aliktuq
tears it	alikta
tears it in several places	aliktuqtaa
tears; *burst into* ___	qiahijuq
tears; *makes* ___ (as in crying)	qulviliuqtuq; qiajuq
tease; *they (two)* ___ *each other*	nanngutiqatigiiktuk; kipaqatigiiktuk
teases him/her/it	kipataa; nangutaa
teases someone	nanngutijuq; nanngudjijuq
teasing partner	kipaqati; nanngutiqati
teaspoon	aluutinnuaq
teenaged boy	inuuhuktuq

teenaged girl	arnaruhiq
teeth; *has no more* ___	kigutaiqtuq
teeth; *works on his/her/its* ___; *brushes* ___	kiguhiqijuq
telescope	qin'ngun/qin'ngut/qin'ngutik
telescopic sight	qin'ngun/qin'ngut/qin'ngutik
tells a legend or story	unipkaaqtuq
tells him/her/it	uqaallautijaa
tells him/her/it to do something	pitqujaa
tells someone to do something	pitquijuq
temper; *never loses his/her* ___	mamiahujuittuq
ten	qulit
tender meat	aqilummaaq
tender; *is* ___	aqittuq
tent	tupiq
tent canvas	tupikhaq
tent frame	qanak
tent pole; *upright* ___	napariaq
tent; *has set up a* ___	tupiqtuq
tent; *horizontal ridgepole of a* ___	nalariaq
tent; *making a* ___	tupqijuq
tent; *sets up a* ___	tupiqtuqtuq; napajuq
tern; *Arctic* ___	imitqutailaq
terrain; *rocky* ___	ujaraktujuq
testicle	igjuk *(d. igjuuk)*
thank you	quanaqqutit (d. *quanaqqutik*, pl. *quanaqquhi*)
thank you very much	quanaqpiaqqutit (d. *quanaqpiaqqutik*, pl. *quanaqpiaqquhi*)
thankful; *always so* ___ *for*	quanaqpakpuuq
thankful; *is* ___	qujahuktuq; quanaqtuq
thankful; *is* ___ *to him/her/it*	qujagijaa
thanks	quana
thanks him/her/it	qujagijaa

that one	talva
that one (unspecified)	taimna
that one down there	kanna
that one over there	taingna
that one there	taamna
that; *like* ___	taimaatun; taimaa
thawed; *already* ___	auktuqtaaqtuq
thawed; *is* ___ *out*	aumajuq
thawed; *is not completely* ___	auktuttiaqhimaittuq
thawed; *is not quite* ___	aukhittiaqhimaittuq
thawed; *is properly* ___	aukhittiaqhimajuq
thawing it out	mahakhiqtuq
thaws	auktuqtuq
theatre; *movie* ___	piksasuurvik (*from "picture show"*)
them; *all of* ___	tamaita
there; *over* ___	taavani
there; *that one* ___	taamna
these right here	hamma
these three (or more)	ukuat
these two	ukuak
thick; *is* ___	ivjujuq
thickens by itself	ivjuhiliqtuq
thicker; *makes it* ___	ivjuhiliqtaa
thigh	qukturaq (d. *quqtuqqak*)
thimble	tikiq
thinks	ihumajuq
thinks about him/her/it	ihumagijaa
thinks about something	ihumaliuqtuq
thinks bad thoughts	ihummarluktuq
thirsty; *is* ___	imiruktuq; immiqijuq
this one	ukua
this one here	una
this place	hamna

this; *do it ___ way*	imaa; imaatun
this; *like ___*	imaatun; imaa
thorn	kakillarnaq
thought	ihuma
thread	ivalukhaq
thread; *spool for ___*	ivalukhaun
threads a needle	nuvihijuq
three	pingahut
three; *catches/gets ___ of something*	pingahuraaqtuq
three; *does something ___ times*	pingahuiqtuqtuq
throat	iggiaq
through; *goes ___* (of arrow, bullet, etc.)	anikkurijuq
throws it away	igitaa
throws something	iqqaqtuq
thumb	kublu
thumps (of a rabbit's foot)	tukkaliqtuq
thunder	kalluk
thunder; *it is starting to ___*	kallulaqijuq
thunder; *there is ___*	kalluguqtuq; kalluktuq
Thursday	Hitammiut
tickle; *gives a ___ing sensation*	quinangnaqtuq
ticklish; *feels ___*	quinaktuq
tide	ulipkaaqtaa
tide is out (low tide)	imaiqtittuq
tied; *is ___ with a rope or chain*	ipiqtuq
tied; *is ___ up* (a package)	qiliqtuq
ties it up (a package)	qiliqtaa
tight	hukattuq
tight; *is ___* (of clothes)	kapittuq; hukangajuq
time; *a long ___ ago*	ingilraan
time; *at that ___*	taimuuna
time; *at that ___* (in distant past)	taimani

time; *kills* ___	tuninnguiqtirijuq
time; *last* ___	kingullirmi
time; *some* ___ *ago*	imani
time; *what* ___ *is it*	humunngaqqa
timid animal	niviuqtujuq
tip	nuvuk
tired; *is* ___	unaguqtuq
tired; *is not* ___	unaguittuq
tissue	kakkiijaun/kakkiijaut/kakkiijauti
tobacco pouch	tipaakuun
toboggan	qamauk; hituaqtuutit
toboggan; *travels by* ___ *or sled*	qamauktuqtuq
today	ublumi
toe	inugaq (pl. *inukkat*)
toe; *big* ___	putuguq (d. *putukkuk*)
together; *all* ___	atauttikkun
together; *are doing something all* ___	atauttikkuuqtut
together; *puts them* ___	atauttimuktait
toilet	anarvik
toilet paper	iquutikhaq
toilet training (traditional form)	kinittijuq
tomcod	uugaq
tomorrow	aqagu
tomorrow evening	unnuffaaqqat
tomorrow morning	qaukpat
tomorrow; *day after* ___	aqaguani
tongue	uqaq
tonight	unnukpan
tools	hanalrutit
tooth	kigun (pl. *kigutit*)
tooth (back molar)	iqhiqpak
tooth; *canine* ___	tuluriaq

tooth; *incisor (front)*	hivuaq
tooth; *pulls out his/her/its* ___	kigutaijaqtaa
toothache; *has a* ___	kigulliuqtuq
toothpaste	kigutigikhaun/kigutigikhaut/ kigutigikhauti
top; *on its* ___	qaangani
top; *the* ___	qaanga
toss; *are playing skin* ___	avataaqtaqtut
touches him/her/it	kahaktaa
touches; *barely* ___ *him/her/it*	kahakaffuktaa
towards	mikhaanun
towel	allarun/allarut/allaruti
toy	ulapqiujaq; piujaq
toy; *plays with a* ___	ulapqiujaqtuq
toy cup/dishes	qallutaujaq
track	tumi
track; *finds* ___	tuffijuq/tuphijuq
tracks an animal	tuvjaqtuq
tracks; *follows* ___	tuvjaqhijuq; tuvjaqtuq
tracks; *looks for* ___	tuffiuqtuq; tumihiuqtuq
trades it	himmauhiqtaa
tradition	pitquhiq
trail	apquhiniq
trail made by man or sled	init
trail; *follows a human-made* ___	iniruajuq
trail; *follows an animal's* ___	tuvjaqtuq
trains dogs by adding them to a dog team	unaguqtaiqhajait
trains him/her/it	ajuiqhajaa
trains someone/something to be a leader	hivuliqtiliuqtuq
translates	numiktirijuq
translator	numiktiriji
trap; *leghold* ___	naniriaq

trapline	naniriaqturvik
travelling by himself	kihimmiuqtuq
travels	aullaaqtuq
travels against the wind	algumuuqtuq
travels by sea	tarjukkuuqtuq/tariukkuuqtuq
travels by sled	aalliaqtuqtuq
travels by toboggan	qamauktuqtuq
travels with the wind	uqumuujuq
treasurer	maniliqiji
tree	napaaqtuq
tree; *branch of a* ___	ihaqutaq (pl. *ihaqutait*)
tree; *spruce* ___	qiuvik; qijuvik
tries hard	akhuuqtuq
tries it on	uuktuqtaa
trim on a cloth parka cover	ikhiq (*see* qupak)
trim; *delta braid* ___	qupak
trim; *fur* ___ *around cuffs*	airutik
trim; *fur* ___ *around parka hood*	puhitaq
trim; *fur* ___ *on parka*	hinikhaq
trip; *takes him/her/it along on a* ___	aullautijaa
trousers	qarliik
trout	ihuuq
trout; *big lake* ___	ihuuqiq
trout; *medium-sized lake* ___	ihuuriktuq
truck	akhaluun/akhaluut/akhaluuti
trustworthy	ukpirnaqtuq
truth; *it is the* ___	ilumuuqtuq; iqunngittuq
try harder!	akhun
T-shirt	iluvruaq
Tuesday	Aippiut
tumpline	kakautaq
turn it on!	ikidjuk

turned on; *is* ___	ikumajuq
tusk	tuugaaq
twice; *does it* ___	malruiqtuqtuq
twins	malriak/malrik
twins; *has* ___	malrijuq
twisted; *is* ___	qipingajuq
twists it	qipijaa
two	malruk
two at a time; *are going* ___	malruiqtaqtut
two; *catches or gets* ___ *of something*	malruraaqtuq

ugly; *is* ___	pinniittuq
ulu/knife/axe blade	kiinaa
unable; *is* ___	ajuqtuq
unable; *is* ___ *to manage alone*	aqtuliqtuq
uncle on father's side	pangnaarjuk
uncle on mother's side	angak
under	ataani
under; *passes* ___ *him/her/it*	ataaguuqtaa
undershirt	ilupaaq
understand; *cannot* ___	kangiqhilimaittuq; kangiqhimanngittuq; uingajuq
understand; *is easy to* ___	uingairnaqtuq; kangiqhihurnaqtuq
understand; *makes him/her/it* ___	hivuniqhipkaqtaa
understands	uingaiqtuq
understands him/her/it	kangiqhijaa; uingaiqtaa

undressed; *is* ___	aannuraangiqtuq; uhiqtuq; uhin'ngajuq
undresses	aannuraangijaqtuq; uhiqtiqtuq
unfortunate; *was* ___	qutaktuq
ungrateful; *is* ___	qujajuittuq
unhappy; *is* ___	quviahunngittuq
uninhabited place	inuilaq
unison; *in* ___	atauttikkun
unkind; *is* ___	palvitujuq
unloading place	niudjivik; apurvik; tulagvik
unloads	uhiijaqtuq
unpleasant; *becomes* ___	quvianaittuq
unseen (a spirit)	hunngittuq
unstitched; *becomes* ___	kiluaqtuq
unties it	qilirniiqtaa
upright; *is* ___	napaaqtuq
upright; *sets it* ___	makitaa
upward	qunmun/qunmut
urinates	quijuq
urine	quq
urine; *strong* ___	itiruq/itirurni
us; *all of* ___	tamapta
us; *both of* ___	tamamnuk
us; *the three or more of* ___	uvagut
used; *is* ___ *up*	nunguttuq
uses	atuqtaa
uses	atuqtuq; -tuq
uses it up	nungutaa
uterus	igliaq

vagina	uttuk
valley	naqhaq
vein	taqak
ventures inland	aavaqtuq
vertebra	kuapigaq *(pl. kuapikkat)*; qimirluk
vest	aingittuq
vicinity	qanilruq
vicinity; *in the* ___	qanilrumi
visible; *is* ___	nuitajuq; takunnaqtuq
visible; *is not* ___	takunnaittuq
visitor from out of town	aquihimajuq
visits	pulaaqtuq
visits from another place	aquijuq
voice	nipi
vomits	miriaqtuq
voracious; *is* ___	uningajuq

wades into water	naluktuq
wags/moves its tail (land mammals)	pamirraaqtuq/pamiqhaaqtuq *(see papiqqiqijuq)*
waist	qitiq
wait at a seal's breathing hole; *was told to* ___	nikpaqujaanga
waits	nutaqqijuq; utaqqijuq

waits at a seal's breathing hole	nikpaqtuq; nippaqtuq
waits for him/her/it	utaqqiuqtaa; nutaqqiuqtaa
waits for someone to come home	aittiijuq
waits for someone/something to appear	nuittiijuq
wakes him/her/it up	tupaaqtaa
wakes him/her/it up (in a rough manner)	tupakhaqtaa
wakes up	tupaktuq
wakes up early	tupagiaqtuq
walking; *has difficulty* ___	pihudjarluktuq
walks	pihuktuq
walrus	aiviq
walrus; *gets a* ___	aiviqtuq
wanders	hangujuq
want; *does not* ___	pijumanngittuq
wants	pijumajuq
wants it	pijumajaa
wants more	pijumaffaaqtuq/taitaiphaaqtuq/ taitaiphaaqtuq (*childish speech*)
wants; *always* ___ *to*	pijumatujuq
war; *are fighting a* ___	angujaktut
warm; *keeps* ___	uqquujuq
warm; *no longer* ___	uquiqtuq/uqquiqtuq
warm; *not* ___	uquittuq/uqquittuq
warm; *weather is* ___	kialaqijuq/qaajurnaiqtuq
warming up; *is* ___ *from being cold*	aukhiqtuq
warms himself/herself/itself	aukhiqtuqtuq
warms up	uunnaalaqijuq; auktuqtaqtuq
warrior	angujakti
wart	unnguq
washes him/her/it	uaqtaa
washes himself/herself/itself	uaqtuq; uaqtiqtuq
washes something	uaqhijuq

washing machine	uaqhin/uaqhit/uaqhiti
wasp	milukattak
watch; *wrist* ___	upluqhiun/upluqhiut/upluqhiuti (*also* ubluqhiun)
watches	tautuktuq
water	imaq
water flowing down	qurluaqtuq
water is rushing down	qurluqtuq
water truck	imiqtaun/imiqtaut/imiqtauti
water; *drinkable* ___	imiq
water; *fetches* ___	imiqtaqtuq
water; *fetches snow to make* ___	aniutaqtuq
water; *good, fresh* ___	imariktuq
water; *melts ice or snow to make* ___	immiuqtuq
water; *shallow* ___	ikkalruq/itkalruq
water; *snow to make* ___	aniu
water; *there is open* ___ *or a lead in the ice*	uittuq
waterfall	qurluq
wave	tagjaaq; malik
wave breaks against the shore	hiqqaqtuq
waves are cresting; whitecaps	qagaaqtuq
waves; *there are* ___	tagjaaqtuq; malliqtuq
wax	patqujaq
way; *in this* ___	imaa; imaatun
way; *is in the* ___	apqutailliutaujuq
we; the two of us	uvaguk
weak; *is* ___	hakugiittuq
weak; *is too* ___ *to manage alone*	aqtuliqtuq
wears out	amiiqtuq; nunguqhuqtuq; alaiqtuq
weasel	tiriaq
weasel; *young* ___	tiriajaaq
weather	hila

weather is warm	kialaqijuq/qaajurnaiqtuq
weather; *bad* ___	hilarluk/hilaluk
weather; *really nice* ___	hilaqqiqtuq
weaves	nuviqhaqtuq
Wednesday	Pingattiut
weight for a fish net	titqaun/titqaut/titqauti; kivvin/kivvit/ kivviti
welcome; *you're* ___	takiunniit/takiunniin
well; *does not do things* ___	pidjarluktuq; pimmarluktuq
well; *does not function* ___	qutangajuq
well; *does things* ___	pimmariktuq
well; *fits* ___	nalaumajuq
well; *stay* ___	naammadjavutit (d. *naammadjvutik,* pl. *naammadjavuhi*)
went by (travelling on ice or water)	kitauttuq
west; *in the* ___	uataani
west side	uataa
west wind	ungalaq
Western Arctic Inuit	Ualinirmiut
westward	uanmun
whale; *beluga* ___	qilalugaq
whale; *bowhead* ___	arviq (*see* arvaaq)
whale; *edible part of* ___ *skin* (**not blubber**)	maktak/maktaaq
whale; *gets a beluga* ___	qilalugaqtuq
whale; *gets a bowhead* ___	arviqtuq
whale; *got a killer* ___	aarluktuq
whale; *killer* ___	aarluk
whale; *young beluga* ___	qilalugaaq
whale; *young bowhead* ___	arvaaq (*see* arviq)
what	huna (d. *hunak;* pl. *hunat*)
what (the direct object of a sentence)	humik/humin
what are you doing	hulivin/hulivit

INUINNAQTUN TO ENGLISH

what is he/she/it doing	huliva
what is it	hunauva
what is the matter	huva
what's your name	kina atqin; kinauvit; kimik atiqaqqit
wheelbarrow	agjautik
when (in future)	qakugu (*see* qanga)
when (in past)	qanga (*see* qakugu)
where	nani; nauk; humi
where are you from	humiutauvin/humiutauvit
where are you going	humunngauvit; humunngauliqqin/ humunngauliqqit
where did you come from	nakit qaivit
where did you get it from	nakin pijat
where is he/she/it	humiitpa; nauk taimna
where to	humun/humut
where; *from* ___	nakin/nakit; humin/humit
where; *to* ___	hunamun/hunamut
which one (of many)	naliat
which one (of two)	naliak
which two?	kitkuk (*see* kina)
which; *in* ___ *direction*	hunamut/hunamun
whimpers (of dogs)	maraaqtuq
whip; *dog* ___	ungullaun
whispers	ihivjuktuq
whistles	kuummiujaaqtuq/kummiuhaaqtuq
white	qakuqtaq
white; *a* ___ *person*	Qablunaaq
white; *pure* ___	qakkuriktuq
white; *turns* ___	qakuqhijuq
whitefish	kapihilik; aanaakhiiq
whiteout; *there is a* ___	qapalaqijuq
who	kina (d. *kitkuk*; pl. *kitkut*)
who (more than two people)	kitkut (*see* kina)

whole; *is* ___	iluittuq
whom	kinamik; kimik
whose	kia
why	huuq; hukhamun
why; *I wonder* ___	huukiaq; nauna
wick; *candle or lantern* ___	ipiraq
wide; *there is a* ___ *space in between*	ajaniqtujuq
widow	uilgarniq
widow; *is a* ___	uilgaqtuq
widower (man who has lost his wife)	nuliilgaqtuq; nuliangiqtuq
wife	nuliaq
willow leaf	atungaujaq
willow tree	uqpik (*see* avaalaqiaq)
wind	anuri
wind; ___ *is blowing from the east*	nigiqtuq
wind; ___ *is blowing from the north*	kanangnaqtuq
wind; ___ *is blowing from the south*	pingangnalaqijuq
wind; ___ *is blowing from the west*	ungalaqtuq
wind; *a place that is out of the* ___	uqquaq
wind; *east* ___	nigiq
wind; *goes against the* ___	algumuuqtuq
wind; *head* ___	algu
wind; *north* ___	kanangnaq
wind; *south* ___	pingangnaq
wind; *there is a light* ___	anuqhaaqtuq
wind; *travels with the* ___	uqumuujuq
wind; *west* ___	ungalaq
windbreak	uquutaq
window	igalaaq
windscreen	alguilitaq
windy; *is* ___	anuqhiqtuq

windy; *is a little* ___	anurikittuq
windy; *is getting* ___	anuqhilaqiliqtuq
windy; *is no longer* ___	anuraiqtuq
wing (of bird, plane, fly, or mosquito)	iharuq (d. *ihaqquk*, pl. *ihaqqut*)
wins a game	akimajuq
wins it	taktaa; takhijaa
wins something	takhijuq
wins; *always* ___	akimajuktuq
winter	ukiuq
winter has arrived	ukiuqtuq
winter; *spends the* ___	ukiijuq
wipes him/her/it	allaqtaa
wipes something	allaqhijuq
wolf	amaruq (pl. *amaqqut*)
wolf; *gets a timber* ___	aarluktuq
wolf; *timber* ___	aarluk
wolf; *young* ___	amaruaq
wolverine	qavvik/qalvik
wolverine; *young* ___	qalviaq/qalvaaq
woman	arnaq
woman; *goes after a* ___	arniqijuq
woman; *has sex with a* ___	arnaqtuqtuq
woman; *married* ___	uilik
woman; *old* ___	aaquaq
woman's belonging	arnaqhiun/arnaqhiut/arnaqhiuti
womb	igliaq
wood	qijuk/qiuk
wood; *cuts* ___	qidjiuqtuq
wood; *drift*___	tivjaq
wood; *fetches* ___	qiuktaqtuq/qijuktaqtuq
wood; *fetches drift*___	tivjaqtaqtuq
wood shavings; *makes* ___	qijualiuqtuq

word	uqauhiq
work; *does poor* ___	pidjarluktuq; pimmarluktuq
worker	havakti
works	havaktuq; hanajuq
works badly	havvarluktuq
works on it	hanajaa
works well	havvariktuq
worm	qupilruq
worm (specifically caribou noseworm)	tagjuq/tagiuq
worm (specifically pinworm)	quaqtaq
worm (specifically tapeworm)	qumaq
worries	ihumaaluktuq
worries about him/her/it	ihumaalugijaa
worse; *is getting* ___	ingattaqtuq
wound; *open* ___	iki
wounded; *is* ___	ikilik
woven or knitted item	nuviqhaaq
wraps a scarf around someone's face	ivjaruhiqtuqtaa
wrench	hukatirun/hukatirut/hukatiruti
wrings it out	hivvuqtaa
wrings something out	hivvuqtuijuq
wrinkles (on face)	imuniin/imuniit
wrist	algaun/algaut/algauti
writes	titiraqtuq
writes it	titiraqtaa
writes on it	titirarvigijaa
writes to him/her/it	titiqqitaa
writing paper	titiraakhaq; titiraakhaut/titiraakhaun; alilajuq
writing system	titirauhiq
wrong; *did* ___	ihuinaaqtuq
wrong; *goes the* ___ *way*	kiglukkuuqtuq

wrong ....

wrong; *is* ___	ihuittuq
wrong; *looks* ___	takummarluktuq

yawns	aittauqtuq
year	ukiuq
year; *last* ___	aippaangani
year; *next* ___	aippaagu
year; *the* ___ *after next*	aippaagutqikpat
yeast	publak
yellow	quriiqtaq/qurjiqtaq
yes	hii/iihi'
yes; *says* ___	angiqtuq
yesterday	ippakhaq/ikpakhaq
yesterday morning	ippakhaq ublaami/ikpakhaq ublaami
yesterday; *day before* ___	ippakhaani/ikpakhaani
yoke (for carrying water pails)	akiraun/akiraut/akirauti
you (plural)	iliffi
you (singular)	ilvit

notes